Merciless and wily,
the greatest paintings
grab you in a headlock
and proceed in short
order to rearrange
your sense of reality

5 7 9 10 8 6

Vintage
20 Vauxhall Bridge Road,
London S W1V 2SA

Vintage Classics is part of the Penguin Random House
group of companies whose addresses can be found at
global.penguinrandomhouse.com

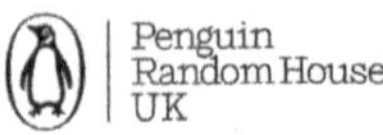

Extract from *The Power of Art* © Simon Schama 2009

Simon Schama has asserted his right to be identified as the author of this
Work in accordance with the Copyright, Designs and Patents Act 1988

The edition *The Power of Art* from which this extract is taken was
first published in Great Britain by The Bodley Head in 2009
*The Power of Art* was first published in Great Britain by BBC Books in 2006

This short edition published by Vintage in 2019

penguin.co.uk/vintage

A CIP catalogue record for this book is available from the British Library

ISBN 9781784875671

Typeset in 10.5/14.5 pt FreightText Pro
by Jouve (UK), Milton Keynes
Printed and bound in Great Britain by Clays Ltd, Elcograf S.p.A.

Penguin Random House is committed to a sustainable future for our
business, our readers and our planet. This book is made from Forest
Stewardship Council® certified paper.

# Art

## SIMON SCHAMA

VINTAGE MINIS

# Contents

# What is Art For?

GREAT ART HAS dreadful manners. The hushed reverence of the gallery can fool you into believing masterpieces are polite things, visions that soothe, charm and beguile, but actually they are thugs. Merciless and wily, the greatest paintings grab you in a headlock, rough up your composure and then proceed in short order to rearrange your sense of reality.

This wasn't why you'd come in out of the rain, was it? There you were, standing in a museum on a Sunday afternoon, ready for a nicely measured dose of beauty – time innocently spent with the wizardry of two-dimensional illusions. Can't you just taste those strawberries on their silver platter? Can't you just smell those pines on a tawny Provençal hillside? Can't you just hear the belching of the Dutch drunks? Can't you just feel that watered silk, the glossy flank of that stallion? No you can't, but still, nothing wrong with imagining, bingeing on the eye-candy, surrendering to the fancy? You settle into the routine, let the colour come to you, walk your eye around the design. Perhaps you do the headset shuffle: sidle, stare, listen, walk; sidle, stare, listen, walk, your attention commanded by the soothingly authoritative voice, a male voice in an expensive suit, the wisdoms toffishly enunciated and thoughtfully rationed so that you don't get too tired for the visit to the gift shop.

But then for some reason you go off-piste; round a corner, beyond the headset zone, and it happens: the peculiar bit. Isn't there something unsettlingly off-kilter about Cézanne's bowl of apples, the way they're sitting askew on the table? For that matter, the tabletop itself seems up-tilted from the horizontal, inviting a giddy slide – a movement that never quite starts, but never quite stops either. What's going on? Or those eyes of Rembrandt's staring from the collapsed pudding of a face? Such a cliché, such a tired joke, such a sentimental projection: the looker looked at. All the same, you can't help but go on staring, feeling accosted, implicated, as though it's somehow all your fault. Sorry, Rembrandt. The people in the gallery disappear. The gallery wall disappears. You're in the hands of some cheap stage hypnotist. You snap out of it, move on and glance – well, why not – at that peachy Titian nude laid out before the swelling hills and, oh-oh, something starts to happen, and not just in your eyeballs. Or you stand dutifully before a Cubist collage, the kind of thing you've never quite got, and still can't see the point of, at least not from the pleasure point of view – but what the hell? You give it a go, and before you know it some piece of your brain starts to do a little dance to the strumming of that guitar, and fragments of newspaper and half-obscured pipes and edges and flats and planes all start to exchange places without so much as asking permission, moving in and out of focused resolution, and you discover you quite like it. You've been nailed again, eye-popped. Life has just been adjusted.

The power of art is the power of unsettling surprise. Even when it seems imitative, art doesn't so much duplicate the familiarity of the seen world as replace it with a reality all of its own. Its mission, beyond the delivery of beauty is the disruption of the banal. Its operational procedure involves the retinal processing of information, but then throws a switch and generates an alternative kind of vision: a dramatised kind of seeing. What we know or remember of sunsets and sunflowers and the form they take in Turner's or van Gogh's paintings seem to exist in some parallel universe – and it's not at all obvious which is the more vivid, the more real. It's as though our sensory equipment has been reset. So it's not surprising that sometimes, in the power surge, we get shocked.

But television doesn't like to be inconvenienced by the unanticipated. Filming needs careful planning. Each of our programmes turned on a crisis in the life and career of an artist, a moment of trouble in the creation of a particular painting or sculpture. En route to that climactic moment, though, we looked at other works, and lurking among them would often be something that threw me completely off balance. A picture I'd blithely thought of as a warm-up act for the big number, seen first-hand rather than through the wan medium of a printed reproduction or a dim memory, suddenly threatened, unnervingly, to be the main feature. Chastened, reeducated, I'd throw a small tantrum, want the programme turned inside out to make room for the epiphany. Directors would hear me out and try not to roll their eyes. Sometimes room would be made for this usurper, sometimes not.

There was, for instance, van Gogh's *Tree Roots and Trunks* (pages 344–5), painted during the last weeks of his life in the summer of 1890. Ostensibly a vole's eye view of densely knotted vegetation, the frantic patterning of the gnarled wood and choking greenery is so visually claustrophobic that it shuts us off from any possibility of landscape. Spatially and psychologically we get no relief, not least because the roots, some of them claw-like and skeletal, others metallic and mechanical, have been monstrously magnified, while trapped within their cage are miniaturised trees. Up is down and down up, far is near and near far. What we are really looking at, then, is a calculated image of disorientation, the painter's extruded ganglia bolting through the space.

Nothing like this had ever dared present itself as a painting before. But in the Van Gogh Museum in Amsterdam, among the iris and sunflower big hitters, no one pays it much heed. There's little call for the postcard, and unless you wanted to strangle someone, you wouldn't want it as a silk scarf.

Then, just when I thought I'd seen them all, there was the Turner surprise. On a misty, late autumn afternoon we were filming at Petworth House in Sussex, home of the Earl of Egremont, one of Turner's most hospitable patrons. At the top of the house was the locked door of a library that had been given over to the painter to use as his studio. The custodian was generous enough to let me go through that door, and there were the book-lined walls much as Turner would have seen them – or, rather, ignored them as he worked; there, too, an easel set up in the place he favoured. As the November fog drew in, so did the whisper of his ghost, which may be why I was set up to see in a little painting in the long gallery downstairs something more than the *View of Chichester Canal* by which it was known to the Victorians. It's one of a sequence of four views in and around Petworth that Turner painted as wall panels, but they're hardly matter-of-fact topography. The park itself is drenched in rosy fairyland radiance, as stags, antlers locked, battle like some mythical incarnation of bewitched warriors.

So does that church on the horizon tell us we are somewhere near Chichester, or perhaps somewhere altogether different – inside the ageing painter's romantically fateful sense of the journey of life, for example? The scene is washed by such an unearthly light that the suspicion that the canal is something other than an expeditious route for lumber or nails becomes irresistible. In a tubby little rowing boat sits a small man in a dark coat and battered hat, very much as the painter was famously wont to do. So perhaps this picture is not a Turner but Turner. In 1827–8, when the painting was made, Turner had arrived at his own middle age. At right-angles to the picture plane – the imaginary window through which we look – a ghostly vessel sails directly down the canal towards us, mysteriously powered since its sails are furled and there's no sign of towing. This ship is no more a workaday sailing barge than Captain Ahab's Pequod was a blubber factory. Black masts reflected in the water, the ship glides towards us in the glimmer, ominous and inevitable. *Chichester Canal*, then, turns out to be an allegorical self-portrait, smuggled into the gallery of Turner's most powerful patron in the guise of a landscape; a cheeky, touching move.

And then, most unnerving of all, there was the apparition in Valletta, Malta. At the end of a long room, the Oratory of the Knights of the Order of St John, in a cathedral where the walls writhed with overwrought wooden carving, and whiskered defunct warriors lay recumbent on tombs glittering with mother-of-pearl mosaic, Caravaggio, then a convicted murderer, depicted (as his get-out-of-jail-free token) the decapitation of the already dead saint John the Baptist. The figures are life size, and painted with such unnerving clarity that they seem to be unbound by any sort of separating frame. We feel we could walk to them at the end of the room, up on their stage overlooking the oratory. The picture is asymmetrically divided. On the left, gathered in a semicircle, is a group of figures, most of whom personify the traditional virtues of art: heroic beauty, gravity, authority. But they are about to engage in butchery, sawing through a dead neck. On the right of the painting is nothing except a rope dangling in the prison yard gloom, while two jailbirds corkscrew their necks through a barred window for a look. One of them bears a resemblance to the criminal painter, but Caravaggio is more emphatically present in the blood oozing from the martyr's neck, which forms itself into a signature; this is one of only two pictures that he ever signed. So the painting perpetuates horror; the artist signs himself in as a culprit; we, his own captives, attempt a look, torn between appalled recoil and stupefied admiration.

All three of these masterpieces not only register the presence of their makers, as if inviting – or daring – us to make a direct connection with them, they crucially feature the artists themselves within a creative drama: van Gogh, the manically enraptured painter of burgeoning nature throttled by his own creations; Turner, the meditative poet of the comings and goings of life; Caravaggio, the devout Christian and criminal, who understands the redemption of blood because he has direct experience of spilling it. In these moments of self-dramatisation, the artist, under extreme pressure, undertakes a work of supremely ambitious scope in which his own most essential beliefs are embodied and creates a work that seeks to change the world.

This is not the norm. A great deal of supremely accomplished art has been created by artists who have preferred self-effacement to heroic self-dramatisation, and who have wanted more modest goals for their work: the imitation of nature; the representation of beauty, or both at the same time. But since the Renaissance the most ambitious artists have wanted to be something grander than laboriously ingenious craftsmen-copyists. In their own eyes they are makers, not fakers. And they have been keen to throw off the condescension of patrons who regarded them as little more than ornamental crafts-men. 'He thinks he's Lord of the World,' Gianlorenzo Bernini's own mother complained to the Pope. And for such lordly creators, possessed in their own minds of a spark of divinity, it was important that their art be acknowledged as noble; akin to philoso-phy, poetry or religion: a human necessity rather than an optional luxury. That impassioned convic-tion led them to assert the authority and power of art in the face of complacency from the holders of institutional power: popes, aristocrats, bureaucrats, moneyed patricians and their tame critics. So the way the drama of their creative life (written by themselves or by biographers) unfolded was typi-cally combative: a conflict with obtuse patrons or their lackeys, the cowardly and conceited critics. The acts in the play are presented as ordeals over which the resolute but bloodied art-maker, pos-sessed of his bright vision, may triumph even as he himself goes under.

It's a professional tic of art historians to write off these dramas of the moment of creation as so much stale rehashing of the romantic fantasies of the tor-mented artist; the corniest story in the book of the muse; a modern platitude about the artistic tem-perament that the old masters would have found unrecognisable. And of course it's quite true that for every van Gogh there's an imperturbable Cézanne;

for every Jackson Pollock, a Matisse; for every painter driven by furies, countless more who have gone to work and lived their lives in a state of disciplined serenity. But the story of the saturnine artist contemptuous of convention, conscious of god-like powers, prey to melancholy, quick to take offence, at odds with short-sighted or vain patrons, embattled with rivals whose mediocrity is matched only by their malice, begins centuries before the Romantics of the 19th century. It begins, in fact, almost as soon as there is any writing about Renaissance artists at all – with Benvenuto Cellini, the goldsmith, sculptor and autobiographer, and with Giorgio Vasari's contemporary biography of Michelangelo.

Of Michelangelo's divine powers Vasari leaves us in no doubt. He has been sent by God himself to earth to exemplify perfection in every form of art: painting, sculpture and architecture. When workers see one of his cartoons they pronounce it more divine than human. He argues with popes and dukes, achieves Herculean labours in painting the Sistine frescoes atop his famous scaffolding. And Vasari implies that Michelangelo was conscious of his own superhuman powers, since during his months in the Carrara marble quarries he contemplated emulating the ancients by carving a colossal image of himself in the mountains.

It was, in fact, the stupendous versatility and

superhuman prowess of Michelangelo that provoked Cellini to write his own extravagant autobiography, *Vita* (1558–66). The latter's masterwork, the bronze *Perseus and the Head of Medusa*, 1545–54, was made for a place in the Loggia dei Lanzi in Florence, where the dripping, severed head of the Gorgon (a technical achievement of such difficulty, as Cellini was at pains to point out, that his contemporaries said it couldn't be done) deliberately confronts Michelangelo's *David*. Every time Cellini can possibly invoke Michelangelo's praise for his own work he does, making sure that the goldsmith would always be thought about by posterity in the same breath as the greatest of the Renaissance masters. The immortality would rub off.

There's a difference, though. Vasari's presentation of Michelangelo is of the austere man-god up on his scaffold, loftily remote from the failings of common clay. Cellini's version of himself, on the other hand, is all too human: a diabolical incarnation of fleshly appetites, the first in a line of artists who imagined that their gift put them beyond the conventions governing lesser mortals. One of his first memories of himself is as a toddler grasping a scorpion by its claws and gleefully dangling it in front of his horrified grandfather. True or false, we'll never know – but from the start it's evident that Cellini wants to cast himself as someone who laughs at the fears of the mediocre and the pusillanimous. There is nothing, then, that Benvenuto won't or can't do. As well as goldsmith and sculptor, he is musician, poet, soldier, swordsman, cannoneer. To say sex and violence run riot in his pages is to understate the truth. Cellini is an unrepentant, outlandish orgiast, consuming men, boys, women, girls, whores, wives – pretty much anyone and anything going. With some women he is brutal, even sadistic. One of his mistresses, Catarina, has the temerity to get married, so Cellini takes a treble revenge, cuckolding her husband, forcing her to pose for hours in an unnaturally painful position and then beating her up. As regards his killings and multiple violent assaults, he is not only unapologetic, but evidently relishes the detailed telling of the deeds. Quick to take offence when he thinks his honour has been impugned, he has no compunction about telling popes and princes just where to get off when he has a mind to.

Running through the compulsively appalling tale is Cellini's sense of his own appetites and impulses as indivisible. The Benvenuto who stabs people in the neck and hauls young boys off to bed is the same Benvenuto who has what it takes to make unimaginable marvels in bronze. Or so he wants us to believe. He boasts, after all, that he would prefer to kill his enemies by art rather than by the sword – but the instinct to annihilate the doubters and jeerers was the same. So his life unfolds as a series of flung gauntlets that Cellini picks up and throws in the teeth of his rivals with demonic energy. And those Herculean triumphs achieved against impossible odds begin with the feat of writing the autobiography itself while under house arrest, in his fifties, for acts of sodomy. Denied pen and ink, he uses, so he tells us, what is to hand: a solvent of rubbed brick dust to make ink, and a splinter of wood from his door as a writing instrument. Thus the tale of the bloody-minded hero, supremely confident of his own powers and supremely indifferent to the small-minded mortals who get in his way, can begin.

The famous climax of the story occurs at the moment when Cellini's bronze *Perseus* is ready for casting, only for the sculptor to fall so sick that he becomes convinced of his imminent death. At least, he believes, his work will survive and be recognised as the equal of Michelangelo's *David*. Something, however, goes terribly wrong with the molten metal, which 'curdles', the base of the alloy congealing. A man bent like an 'S' appears to the feverish master on his sickbed, intoning the doom of his great project. In response to the devilish apparition, Cellini leaps from the bed to rescue the work of nine years from disaster. The scene becomes operatic. A furnace explodes; a great rainstorm bears down on the beleaguered workshop. Two hundred pewter platters and kitchen pots are hurled on to the furnace to get the molten liquid to the right consistency. Amidst all this wildness the super-artist stays cool and, of course, the *Perseus* is rescued, made perfect – the *Vita* ensuring that no one who saw it would ever forget the superhuman manner of its creation.

Not all artists suffer from delusions of megalomania of Cellini's calibre. But there is a tradition – from Caravaggio to Mark Rothko – of artists who have self-consciously cast themselves as heroic champions of the conversionary power of art. Each created a work under severe stress – from patrons (Rembrandt), from the political moment (David, Turner, Picasso), from a sense of self-vindication (Caravaggio, Bernini) and from their own exacting sense of what art should be and do (van Gogh, Rothko). Each of those works tested the capacity of the artist not just to fulfil the terms of his commission, but to transcend it.

In rising to the occasion, each of the artists, as it happened, turned a new page in the history of art, to produce something unprecedented. In some cases, such as Rembrandt, Turner and Picasso, they created momentous history paintings, so massively complete an answer to the challenge of the moment that they could never be repeated, not by themselves and much less by apostles or imitators.

So these dramas are histories as much as art histories (and in any case, the distinction has sometimes been lost on me). At stake in their success or failure were the things that go to the heart of our individual and shared existence: salvation, freedom, mortality, transgression, the state of the world and the state of our souls. All of these works are, in their several and incommensurable ways, shockingly beautiful, and there's nothing shameful or trivial about that. But their creation – even, or especially, in the case of the abstract artist Rothko – was not fundamentally driven by the reach for aesthetic effect. Famously, Picasso (who was not allergic to beauty) put it most trenchantly and self-righteously when he said that 'paintings are not done to decorate apartments; they are weapons of war'. The fact that for much of the rest of his career after *Guernica*, he did little else but produce stuff that served perfectly well as interior decoration suggests how atypical these dramatic episodes of consummate public vocation were. But when they happened, in a bolt of illumination, the works tell us something about how the world is, how it is to be inside our skins, that no more prosaic source of wisdom can deliver. And when they do that they answer, irrefutably and majestically, the nagging question of every reluctant art-conscript, be they nine or fifty-nine, who's been dragged through a museum door, leaden-footed, sighing heavily, wistfully hankering for the football results or the fashion sales: 'OK, OK, but what's art really for?'

# Caravaggio



FROM THE START, there are only two things you need to know about Michelangelo Merisi da Caravaggio: that he made the most powerfully physical Christian art that has ever been painted, and that he killed someone. Do these two facts have the slightest connection? I should hope not, the art historians will tell you, horrified by the crassness of the question. The fact of the painter's crime, they will say, is merely a sensationalist footnote to his career as maker of pictures. Beware romantically reading the art from the life, or for that matter vice versa; the one has nothing whatsoever to do with the other.

But then you look at Caravaggio's shocking painting of himself as the severed head of the Philistine giant Goliath. And you see something that had never been painted before and would never be painted again: a portrait of the artist as ogre, his face a grotesque mask of sin. It's an image of unsparing self-incrimination and it certainly makes you wonder.

## II

IT'S A COMMONPLACE about Caravaggio's pictures that, more than those of any other artist, the viewer responds to his figures physically. All the same, I wasn't ready to hold in my hand something that Caravaggio had held in his.

'Please,' said the wizened man with the beaky nose and the black cassock, nudging me in the ribs. 'Please, take.' I wasn't in the mood to be nudged. It had been yet another embarrassing day with Caravaggio, attempting to say something that illuminated his drama while painfully conscious that he did his own lighting, thanks very much; and that words were a feeble fluttering thing beside the muscular heft of his painting. In the cathedral oratory at Valletta, my back to *The Beheading of St John the Baptist*, face to the camera, speech had never seemed so redundant. I wanted to be out of the musty dimness of that church. The bar stool at the Ship pub, from which Oliver Reed had terminally tumbled, was calling for an act of homage. I had had my fill of art.

Still, courtesies were called for. Rule number one of location filming is to show proper gratitude to those whose premises you have occupied with the self-important baggage of cable, lights, camera. Besides, the small man in the cassock was giving me a wry grin as he did his poking: 'Please, take.' So I sighed, looked and took. In my hand was an ancient iron key about five inches long. The looped handle end had got furry in the way very old pieces of metalwork do, but the entry end sported massive squared-off teeth. I had used keys like this before when I'd been a Cambridge don and occasionally had to open oak doors with 17th-century locks. But why was I getting this key in the cathedral of the Knights of St John? I smiled uncomprehendingly back at the verger, now vaguely aware I had seen this particular key before. Indeed I had, just two minutes before. The gnomic figure in black now tightly grasped my free hand, as if I were a child and he my schoolteacher, and turned me round to face Caravaggio's painting. And of course, there it was: one of three keys hanging from the belt of the grimly handsome prison officer who was pointing to the basket in which the head of the Baptist was about to be deposited.

Caravaggio, his earliest biographers, Giulio Mancini and Giovanni Baglione, tell us, almost always used live models, and since the figures in the *Beheading* are life-sized, and he had painted the altarpiece *in situ*, there could be little doubt that he had done so in the space in which we were now all standing. He needed the keys – emblems of incarceration – to ramp up the nightmarish claustrophobia that manages to pervade even this huge painting. So he had posed his grizzled model and then, perhaps, asked for a set of keys to hang from the man's belt. The cathedral clergy were probably as accommodating to him as they had been to us, lending whatever was to hand. The key in my hand matched precisely, tooth for tooth, the one in the painting. 'See, yes, see,' said the verger. 'His.' I palmed the blackened thing, then I wrapped my fingers around its abraded shaft. I was nervously shaking hands with a 400-year-old genius-killer.

Caravaggio, the jailbird, was haunting me at the scene of my own venial crime – cutting him down to television size. But then Caravaggio is the most confrontational of painters, with everything calculated to be too close for comfort. His big paintings get in our face like no others because they are designed to rip away the protective distance conferred by high art. A blaze of light catches the figures, but around them is utter blackness swallowing up the comfort zone of art-gazing: frame, wall, altar, gallery. The great breakthrough of Renaissance painting had been perspective, the depth punched through the far side of the picture plane. But Caravaggio is more interested in where *we* are, in the space in front of the picture plane which he makes a point of invading. Looking at the outflung arms of Christ in his

*Supper at Emmaus,* 1600–01, (National Gallery, London), you almost duck to avoid the impact. Caravaggio isn't a beckoner – he's a grabber, a button-holer; his paintings shamelessly come out and accost us, as if he were crossing the street and, oh God, coming our way. 'You *looking* at me?'

This is an artist who enjoys reminding us he's there. Unlike Rembrandt, he never does so by means of formal self-portraits, but got up as some player in one of his own painted performances. The only image we have of him out of character is Ottavio Leoni's drawing, which, with its mane of wiry hair, snub nose and large, piercing eyes, seems (especially in comparison with Leoni's drawings of Caravaggio's better-behaved contemporaries) to charge straight out of its demure format. Why did he like posing for some of his own pictures? It's possible that, 'naked and in need', as Giulio Mancini, the doctor who treated him and became his first contemporary biographer, describes him in his early days in Rome, he was the only model he could afford. (However, this seems unlikely since friends evidently posed for paintings well before Caravaggio had anything like a steady income.) But even if the practice began as a necessity, it went on as a choice. For Caravaggio's self-dramatisation was a calculated gesture, as challenging and aggressive to the conventions of art as the contemptuous sweep of a dirty thumb over his lower lip. Over the fifteen years of his career he appears as a 'sick Bacchus'; as a boy emitting a howl of pain as he's bitten by a lizard; as another screamer – the serpent-coiled face of the monster Medusa at the moment of her death; as a come-hither horn player at the back of a group of winsomely clad musicians; as a frantic bystander getting out of the way of St Matthew's brutal killing; as the curious holder of a lantern that sheds light so that wickedness can be done and destiny fulfilled – the apprehension of Jesus in the garden at Gethsemane; and, most unforgettably, at the very end as that monstrous head of Goliath, eyes bulging in their sockets, mouth agape, drool puddling at the slack lower lip, brow furrowed in stricken bewilderment around the puncturing wound from David's slung stone.

Appearing in one's own history paintings was nothing unusual. Michelangelo painted his own likeness, bearded and intense, as the flayed St Bartholomew in the Sistine Chapel, and Giorgione, whose work Caravaggio is likely to have seen in Venice, is known to have represented himself as David with the head of Goliath. It was one thing, though, to cast yourself as the beauteous hero, the forerunner indeed of the Saviour; quite another to appear as the colossus of depravity and sin. It was, after all, exactly at this moment in history that painters were at pains to present themselves as masters of learning, socially and morally ennobled by their calling, not as lowly craftsmen – and much less as fallen ogres. But then Caravaggio specialised in the unexpected. So he begins his string of self-images as a debauched Bacchus and ends it with a slain Goliath. In between that beginning and that ending every appearance he makes is in the guise of sinner. Now why would he want to do that?

III

IN 1592 THE TWENTY-ONE-YEAR-OLD Caravaggio arrived in Rome, an unknown Lombard from the small town of Caravaggio just eight miles outside Milan. He would leave it in a hurry in 1606, a fugitive from justice. Between those dates he transformed Christian art more completely than anyone since his namesake, Michelangelo.

In so many ways the Roman Church had been waiting for him. Assailed by the northern European Reformation, it was in dire need of a sacred visual drama that simple believers could respond to tangibly as if it were acted out in their presence. Much was at stake. Images were not just an incidental sideshow in the religious war between Catholics and Protestants; they went to the heart of the matter. For Lutherans, the Word written in the Holy Scriptures was everything. Printing had made that word, translated into their vernacular language, available to all believers, enabling literate Christians to have a direct, unmediated personal relationship with their Saviour. The claim of the Roman clergy, from the Pope down to the parish priest, that they alone held the keys to salvation, and that redemption could only be achieved through the mysteries and rituals of which they were the guardians, was dismissed by Lutherans as a wicked and presumptuous fraud. And at the heart of what they perceived as institutionalised deception were images: the pictures and sculptures of saints and madonnas, of the Saviour and even (the most shocking blasphemy, this) of the Heavenly Father himself. These were the idols, the painted mummery, by which the credulous were kept infantile, held in thrall by the Pope of Rome and his minions. They were, thundered the Lutherans, a plain violation of the second commandment, which forbade 'graven images'. So along with the secret distribution of vernacular Bibles, the most dramatic expression of the Protestant revolution was the destruction of images. On to the bonfire they went, in the Netherlands, Germany, England and in the reformed Protestant Swiss cities of Geneva, Basel and Zurich.

Shaken by the scale and fury of the destruction of images, it took little time for the Roman Catholic Church to mount a counter-attack. One of the major issues tackled at the Council of Trent, in its final session in 1561–3, was the role of sacred paintings in inspiring the faithful to worship, venerate and obey. Instinctively as well as intellectually the Church Fathers knew that, since the vast majority of men and women in Europe were illiterate, images were still the most powerful way to instruct the masses and hold their allegiance. To do otherwise was to condemn the poor and unlettered to ignorance, heresy and, ultimately, the damnation of their immortal souls. So instead of backing off from the making of sacred images, they would commission many more. Sensibly, they conceded that there had been abuses and extravagances in some of the art that had found its way into churches: depictions of fabulous wonders done by dubious saints that were little more than fairytales; liberties taken with the likenesses of the Father and the Holy Virgin; even some gross indecencies that made images more like distracting entertainments than objects of reverence. All those corruptions would go. Henceforth, the Council decreed, sacred art would be in the spirit of the Saviour himself: modest and austere. It would forego the seductions and pagan profanities of worldly beauty for the supreme vocation of instilling piety.

The only problem was, no one quite knew what such an art would look like. In 1571, when Caravaggio was born, Michelangelo had been dead for just seven years. He and Raphael had been the only two masters in Rome who had seemed capable of expressing in sculpture and painting one of the Church's central doctrines: that the meaning of the Gospel was God's compassion, embodying his son in human flesh so that his sacrifice could redeem the sins of mankind. Inseparable from this core belief was the emphasis on the Incarnation and Passion as physical experiences. To convey the epic of Christ's body in a manner with which all believers could emotionally identify while still preserving the equally indispensable mystery of divinity was the most challenging element of the Christian painter's vocation. Michelangelo's *Pietà* of 1500, for example, was supremely successful at rising to this challenge. The Madonna is figured as a grieving mother with the broken torso of her son laid across her lap. The fact that the Virgin's features appear, if anything, younger than those of her son is rescued from incongruousness because we recognise transfiguration through divinity into a kind of agelessness.

In their separate styles both Michelangelo and Raphael were capable of reconciling the representation of mortal flesh and immortal spirit. But at the end of the 16th century when, under the papacy of Sixtus V, there was a great renewal of building and teaching timed to culminate in the Holy Year of 1600, and the churches of Rome were in urgent need of compelling images to inspire the faithful, it was embarrassingly unclear who could fill their shoes. The choice was obvious enough: fervent dreams or classical statues? An earlier generation, gripped by visions, had put beauty over nature and had specialised in stylised figures, elongated limbs and torsos, balletically torqued in space and coloured, like shot silk, by a fantasy palette of apricots, purples and rose pinks that seemed to come straight from some High Renaissance runway. At their weirdest and most wondrous the images produced by artists like Rosso Fiorentino and Jacopo Pontormo were unarguably beautiful, but too ethereally unmoored from nature to appeal to anyone not in on the arcane secret. Besides, to the sober Fathers of the Church, who were monitoring post-Trent standards of piety and decency, these Mannerist confections seemed suspiciously sensual.

The alternative was a return to the statuesque classical grandeur and emotional simplicity of Raphael: finely drawn figures, harmoniously disposed in deep space. The only late 16th-century artists with the evident talent to achieve that revival were the Carracci brothers, Agostino and Annibale, the sons of a Bolognese tailor. But until the last two years of the century the Carracci were working in Bologna and remained virtually unknown in Rome. Besides, although Annibale in particular was wedded to what by Roman standards passed for realism, compared with Caravaggio – as a commission in the Cerasi Chapel in the church of Santa Maria del Popolo would make spectacularly clear – even he would seem like the softest, most cherubic idealist.

How could Annibale have known? How could anyone have known what was about to hit them? Caravaggio came out of obscurity, from the peculiarly grim darkness of Spanish-ruled Milan. The city was an embattled citadel, economically and spiritually. Its hardware walked the streets in the shape of swords, daggers and armour; its guns were mounted on the fortifications Leonardo da Vinci had designed for the Sforza dukes. But the most famous general of the faith militant was Carlo Borromeo, guiding light of the Council of Trent. It had been Borromeo whose unimpeachably simple life, even (or especially) as a prince-cardinal, combined with his attention to the poor had returned the Church to its pastoral duty of imitating the life of Christ.

What was wanted for the altarpieces of this newly populist Roman Church, then, were images that were also naturally simple and accessible – the remote grandeur of the Renaissance masters brought down to earth. But the talent available to achieve this was, to put it mildly, limited. Milanese painters such as Antonio Campi and Simone Peterzano certainly did dark and simple in the spirit of Borromeo's austerity, and they did their best with the obligatory nod to the local hero, Leonardo, delivering studiously drawn fruit, flowers and animals into the scenery. If modesty was the intended effect, they succeeded all too well, but it was at the expense of drama. It seems inconceivable that even the most willing worshipper could have looked at an altarpiece by Peterzano, caught his breath and felt he was in the presence of the living Gospel.

Then into Peterzano's workshop some time in the mid-1580s came a stocky, beetle-browed teenager, probably already with something of an attitude. He hailed from a dull region of flat pasture and distant horizons: sheep, mournful avenues of poplars, one standard-requirement local miracle (Virgin appears to country girl), one grand basilica built to honour same, plus the odd fort and villa. But young Michelangelo Merisi (named after the sword-brandishing angel rather than the brush-brandishing genius) was not entirely a social zero. He had connections, albeit of a forelock-tugging kind. His father, Fermo Merisi, had been the architect-builder and household steward to the local marchese, living in Milan while doing the job. But any hope that his two sons might be upwardly mobile had been cut short by his death in the plague epidemic that swept through Milan in 1577. Fermo's widow, Lucia, and her four children had already been sent outside the city, to the small town of Caravaggio, to escape the epidemic. With properties sold up to settle debts, the best the older boys could hope for was the priesthood or some modestly respectable craft or trade. Giovanni Battista would become the priest; Michelangelo the painter.

Art history is constitutionally incapable of discounting influence, but aside from strongly lit figures in dimness, and the simplified cast of characters, it's hard to see much of what became Caravaggio in the example of Peterzano. Had he stayed in Milan, it's possible that he might have remained obscure since he served his time doing what apprentices had to do: grinding colours, dabbing in details. But before he was twenty-one, according to his early biographers, Caravaggio had already become Trouble. He'd run through his small share of the procceds from the sale of his mother's property, and ran around with toughs and whores in a city where street fighting was the favourite pastime. One biographer claims that he killed someone; but more credibly Mancini, the writer closest to Caravaggio's own lifetime, mentions a fight in which a prostitute's face was slashed. Refusing to snitch on whoever had committed the assault, Caravaggio did time in a Milan prison. A pattern had been set.

By the early 1590s Caravaggio had ended up, inevitably, in Rome, one of a restless, buzzing swarm of young artists hungry for work, fame and pleasure, not necessarily in that order. There he led a fly-by-night, testosterone-fuelled existence in rented rooms around the Campo Marzio, where other Lombards lived, drinking themselves stupid in rough-house taverns, abusing passers-by on the street and hunting down the action. Caravaggio's artist mates – Prospero Orsi, Mario Minniti and the architect Onorio Longhi – were no angels themselves, quick to get out their blades and constantly in trouble with the *sbirri*, the papal police. The whole gang of them liked to hang out with working girls, who themselves fought like street cats over territories, customers and the affection of their pimps.

Caravaggio's crowd weren't just hoodlums, though. Many of them were bright, talented and ferociously ambitious. They did fights and tarts, but they also did poetry, music, theatre and philosophy. If they were drunk a lot of the time, it was on ideas as much as on sour wine. They even showed up at lectures put on by Federigo Zuccaro's 'Academy' of San Luca. Zuccaro may have been a mediocre portraitist and history painter, but he'd worked for princes, had drawn Queen Elizabeth I with stupendously flattering mendacity, and now presided over the Guild-turned-'Academy' as though it were a combination of his own court and an assembly of philosophically minded artists. In keeping with the high-minded aspirations of the institution, members were sworn to uphold lofty standards, both in their professional practice and in their personal lives.

Caravaggio is known to have gone to some of the meetings of the Guild-Academy, and later to have been a member. When he died, honour was paid to him by the members. But in his early years in Rome he hardly matched Zuccaro's prescription for the dignified artist, going round as he did in shabby-chic black, holes conspicuously showing. What work he had was hack stuff: routine heads and, since it was supposed to be a northern Italian speciality, fruit-and-flowers details for other artists' history paintings. In fact, Caravaggio was not just good at this second-order rendering of nature, but the best since Leonardo, and much the wittiest. The rosy-cheeked boy with the kiss-me-quick lips and plunging neckline, or Caravaggio's friend the Sicilian painter Mario Minniti at his poutiest, loaded down with a basket full of ripe-and-juicy, may both seem perfor-mances of cloying sweetness. But that, of course, is the point. You look at the dimpled peaches with their fine fuzz and then you look at the winsome youths and it's gigglingly obvious that they are the fruit. Poems and songs being written by the likes of Fran-cesco Marino played on just that clichéd conceit. Touch me. Peel Me. Taste me.

All the same, and despite introductions from influential connections, such as the Marchese and

Marchesa of Caravaggio, no one in a position to employ a young jobbing artist was as yet much impressed with the newcomer from the north. Pandolfo Pucci paid his artists so poorly – and fed them even worse – that he was known as 'Monsignor Salad'. The painter glorying in the name of Anteveduto Grammatica took Caravaggio on for a while to turn out 'heads'. It was only when he joined the shop of the most successful up-and-coming painter of altarpieces and ceilings, Giulio Cesari, that Caravaggio got an opportunity to do what counted: sacred history paintings. He may have assisted Cesari with some of the figures on the unfinished decoration of the vaults of the Contarelli Chapel in the church of San Luigi dei Francesi. But it all came to nothing. Depending on the source, Caravaggio spent some months in hospital either because he'd been kicked by a horse or because he'd fallen sick (or possibly both). By the time he had recovered, Cesari made it plain that he was no longer interested in having him back.

To any dispassionate observer, two years after his arrival in Rome Caravaggio's prospects must have looked dim. But two surviving paintings from this early period don't suggest someone who had lost his way or his faith in his own powers. Quite the contrary, in fact. They suddenly announced the presence of a maverick talent, not least because they feature, bold as brass, Caravaggio himself, and in guises that were not exactly what Zuccaro's Academy of San Luca was hoping for.

Of course, if you had a mind to, you could read *Boy Bitten by a Lizard* as a warning against sexual mischief. Just in case you hadn't cottoned on to the bitten digit and the thorny rose, a smirking local would have told you that on the streets, 'lizard' was slang for 'penis'. The wound inflicted on the saucy lounge-lizard with the flower tucked behind his ear was, then, the bite of the inevitable social disease that visited innocents hooking up with the kind of girls Caravaggio and his pals favoured. Much more important than its snigger value, though, was the work's function as a composite portfolio of all the talents that Caravaggio was pitching. Here was someone who, from the detail of the waterbowl in which his own studio was reflected (making the painting a double-disguised self-portrait), was a dazzling master of illusionist naturalism – the first quality that those in the market for raw young talent would seek. But then the perfectly rendered moment of recoil – body thrown back, facial features contorted in pain, skin flushed with a rush of blood – also advertised a master of body and face language, someone who could make visual the extreme passions in just the way Leonardo had demanded of any truly ambitious history painter. Then there was the way in which the picture was lit: a sharp, intensely concentrated light thrown over the figure. Doubtless it was just another of the countless genre scenes on offer in the market stalls and shops of Rome. Believe it or not, there had been other lizard-biting (and, still more ponderously obvious, crab-biting) pictures. But for those who had eyes to see, this was the work of a stunningly strange virtuoso.

Who got rapidly stranger. Perhaps it was when he got out of hospital that Caravaggio painted his *Sick Bacchus*. The very idea of it, never mind the way it was executed, was an outlandish challenge to the conventions. Bacchus, after all, was not just the god of wine and revelry, but one of the patron deities of dance and song; and as such he had always been depicted as a perpetual youth. Caravaggio, however, turned him into a literally sick joke. The lips are grey, the eyes leering, the skin unnervingly sallow, the overloaded wreath of vine leaves around his brow excessive rather than festive. By painting himself as overdressed party animal the morning after, Caravaggio up-ended the conventions. Instead of taking a model with all his human imperfections and translating him through the ennobling magic of art into the embodiment of perpetual youth, beauty and pleasure, the artist took the mythical deity and turned him into a dressed-up mortal, horribly the worse for wear. It's a picture not of immortality but of its opposite: decay. With filth-rimmed nails he offers us a bunch of grapes, the bloom rendered so perfectly that we can see how far gone to rot they are. And the rot is not especially noble.

It's not *just* a joke; it's a revolutionary statement of intent. The whole point of art, according to its Renaissance theorists, was the idealisation of nature. Caravaggio had just announced that his business would be the naturalisation of the ideal.

Caravaggio brings off this unnerving marriage between the pure and the vulgar with a showy skill that no one had seen in Rome since Raphael. Traditionally, 'low-life' subjects – gypsies or tavern scenes – were given the low-light treatment. And because the old familiar stories of innocents taken down by the wiles of the shifty owed so much to the comedy of the theatre, painters who did that kind of thing treated their canvas like a crowded stage, filling it with hurly-burly knockabout to chuckle your way through. Mindful of their inferior place in the hierarchy of paintings – below histories and portraits – low-lifes were always modest little things, meant to be bought cheaply and hung in a back room. This condescension gave Caravaggio another convention to upset. Instead of the raucous comic crowd, he took a very small cast of characters and painted them near life-size so that they dominate the picture space rather than being swallowed up by a picturesque interior. It's the difference between watching a comedy unfold on a remote stage and having it happen inches away from your face. Instead of dwelling on the crudeness of the characters, Caravaggio washes them in the pellucid glow usually reserved for saints. So a turbaned gypsy fortune-teller, usually the personification of danger and corruption, is invested with almost as much peachy seductiveness as the young man whose palm she lightly fingers. Her chemise is fastened modestly to the throat and, like her turban, it could not possibly be whiter. The cheating young *bravo* about to take down his mark in a game of cards differs from his gullible target only in his dress, the cocky plume (and the hand held behind his back) a sign of his worldliness. When he has a mind to, Caravaggio can do crones and ferocious old ruffians with such up-close relish that you can practically smell the onions and the dried sweat. But by avoiding caricature and holding the action at the moment before the denouement he manipulates suspense and makes the deceptions more credible. The punters are giddy with the beauty of the moment. So are we.

None of it would work without the reality effect that before long would make Caravaggio's reputation. And that startling immediacy owed everything to his strategically calculated lighting. His biographer Giulio Mancini tells us that he used a single, strong light source to illuminate figures. All the anecdotally distracting details of a background were either suppressed into an indeterminate dirty gold or grey-brown ground, or, later in his career, consigned to absolute darkness. Against the neutral ground, Caravaggio's figures stand out with cruel sharpness. They seem to occupy the room; you can feel a pulse, sense a breath. Modern writers such as David Hockney have argued that the crystalline clarity of those figures could only have been achieved with the help of a lens, perhaps a camera obscura that would have projected an inverted image on to a back wall. There is no supporting evidence for this theory, even from writers such as Giulio Mancini and Giovan Pietro Bellori, who describe Caravaggio's working methods. However, there's also no reason to preclude the idea. Caravaggio may have hung out with toughs, but they were clever toughs, and there were many in his circle who would have known about the new optics. And paintings like *Boy Bitten By A Lizard* play with inverted reflections. But, of course, using a lens or a convex mirror (one of the latter actually appears in a painting of the conversion of *Mary Magdalene*) to produce a focused image was one thing; translating it to the canvas with the kind of razor-sharp brilliance that Caravaggio habitually achieved was quite another, especially since he seldom actually drew anything.

That Caravaggio dispensed with preparatory drawing was not just a sign of phenomenal eye-hand coordination; it was tantamount to methodological insubordination. *Disegno* – the word that conveyed both the act of drawing and the conception of a larger design – had been prescribed by all the manuals of art theory and instruction as indispensable to the proper making of art. Drawing wasn't just technique; it was ideology. True, it was possible to invoke the Venetians – above all Titian – to argue that *colore*, colour, was not just an auxiliary element but a major constituent in the composing of pictures. And Caravaggio may well have visited Venice on his way from Milan to Rome in 1592. The most obvious anticipations of the intensity of his lighting and brilliance of colour are in the works of Giorgione and Lorenzo Lotto. But unlike them he was living and working in Rome, not Venice. And Rome was all about drawing. If, in the 1590s, you had walked through the collections of classical statues belonging to the Pope and the cardinals, or wandered among the ruins in and around the Forum, you would have seen eager, aspiring young artists sketching away: the Farnese Hercules, the Laocoön, the Apollo Belvedere. As for the Academy of San Luca, it was a truism that there could be no great monumental art without a rigorous training in the study sketches required for any independent composition.

All of which Caravaggio studiously ignored. No preparatory sketches, much less drawings from the antique, survive – if indeed they were ever done. He posed his models, he eyeballed, he painted. The confidence to do that is all the more breathtaking in that Caravaggio was not really a painter in the Venetian manner like Veronese, who built his compositions from modulated blocks of colour. Caravaggio models his figures quite as solidly and sculpturally as if he had worked for years drawing those classical busts. But he's doing it with just eye and hand. If he wanted some guide contours for the composition, he used either the sharp stub end of his brush or perhaps a small knife to make small incisions on the surface of the canvas (and it was always canvases, never wood panels); the blade and the brush, perfect partners in Caravaggio's studio. With those unorthodox methods, plus a gift for perfect composition, he managed to transform 'inferior' genres into pictures that were monumental and dramatic. They were arresting enough for the picture dealer Constantino Spata (who also happened to be a drinking friend) to show them in his shop in the Piazza San Luigi dei Francesi. And there *The Card Sharps* was seen, and bought by someone who changed Caravaggio's life.

## IV

FRANCESCO MARIA DEL Monte wasn't the richest cardinal in Rome. But with his mere 200-odd retainers and servants he wasn't exactly a church mouse either. His family may not have been in the same league as the grandest aristocratic dynasties – the Farnese, Orsini, Aldobrandini and Colonna – who, loaded with country estates and urban palazzi, divided up Rome among them and took turns at supplying popes. But del Monte had something that nonetheless had made for a spectacular ascent to power and fortune: a connection to the Medici Grand Dukes of Florence. A winning combination of cleric and connoisseur, he had learnt courtly culture from the place and the man who defined it – Urbino and Baldassare Castiglione. Castiglione's book *The Courtier*, 1528, had sketched an ideal type, polished in the graces, learned in arts and sciences, generous, courageous and intellectually accomplished. Del Monte aspired to be all these things, and after he'd met Ferdinando de' Medici, the dynasty's cardinal, and had begun to work for him, he had a chance to show off those gifts and virtues. When Ferdinando succeeded to the Grand Duchy in 1588 he repaid del Monte's loyalty by promoting him to the cardinalship he had just vacated. First del Monte got the hat; then he was ordained as a priest! But this doesn't mean he was impiety dressed in scarlet. Del Monte, like his Medici patron, took an intense interest in the Order of the Oratorians, founded by Filippo Neri, whose mission was to return to the pastoral simplicity of the early Church: a Christianity of the streets and begging bowls. This would matter for Caravaggio.

But you couldn't take Urbino out of del Monte. He was hungry for culture – science and mathematics, as well as music, history, poetry and painting. And one way in which the cardinals of Rome established their place in the aristocratic pecking order was by cultural taste and patronage. Religious power in the Holy City was at this time represented by two factions: the Spanish, severe and high-minded, and the more liberal and worldly French. The Farnese, pro-Spanish and thus bitter enemies of the Medici-French connection, had their stable of artists, soon to include the stellar Carracci. So del Monte was on the lookout for promising talent. All he had to do was cross the street to Spata's art shop to see *The Card Sharps*. When he had seen it he must have known he had struck gold. Caravaggio was made an offer: board and lodging; studio space on the top floor of del Monte's Palazzo Madama; and, best of all, patronage, not only by the Cardinal himself, but by the network of grandees, some secular, some in the Church, who came to the palazzo for concerts, dinners and elegantly high-minded conversation.

Caravaggio moved into the Palazzo Madama some time in 1595 and stayed for six years. Many paintings he did during his time there reflect the heavily exquisite quality of the culture within the Cardinal's walls, drowsily poetic and ambiguously sensual: all lutes and fruits. Del Monte prided himself on his musical taste. He bought precious instruments, commissioned pieces from house composers and collected prize singers, some the sought-after castrati, who would perform madrigals in the emotionally loaded manner of Monteverdi. The favourite subject was – what else – love: love unrequited; love as distraction, torment, rapture. 'You know I love you, you know I adore you. But you do not know that I *die* of you,' sings Caravaggio's friend Mario Minniti, got up 'all'antica' in flimsy, deeply scooped muslin, dreamy, fingers strumming the lute. A vase of late spring and summer flowers stands beside him; a viol on the table lies on the score of the madrigal in question.

Obviously, they don't make cardinals like del Monte any more, for the atmosphere of *The Musicians* is claustrophobically erotic, positively tumescent with anticipation: four barely dressed boys shoehorned into an impossibly tight picture space. It's been said demurely that the crowding is a sign of Caravaggio's erratic grip on composition, with the artist cramming too many figures on to a canvas that had originally carried a different painting. But of course he knows exactly what he's doing. Had he wanted to give the figures more breathing room and depth, he need only have reduced their scale. Awkward physical proximity is precisely the point. It's contact painting: thighs and hands and arms all doing *something*, tuning up, plucking grapes and, in the case of Caravaggio himself, at the back grasping his horn. The fact that the dewy youth on the left comes with a pair of Cupid's wings is hardly more than a nod to allegory, a gesture that is a transparently unconvincing alibi against raised eyebrows in the palazzo. This is, after all, a cardinal's residence. Cupid-Boy has his long eyelashes modestly cast down; the figure at the front, almost on our lap, is studying the score, but then we're exposed to his pale back. Although he's just rehearsing, the Minniti-lutenist has already been so carried away by the passion of the piece that his flushed cheeks, heavy eyelids and red-rimmed eyes tell us he's been weeping. His lips are parted – although, since he's tuning the lute, presumably not in song – so perhaps it's Caravaggio himself whose black eyes and thick-lipped mouth are wide open with the music. The two of them stare straight at us. It's an outrageous flirtation; another of Caravaggio's invitational studies that had begun with the 'sick Bacchus', playing, as he would always love to do, both sides of the frame. Was there ever a moment when he was not conscious of art as a three-way game played by himself, his subjects and us, the onlookers?

V

NO ONE IN ROME did the pull of the stare quite like Caravaggio. But that's because no one was so intelligently *interested* in the power of the stare. And what Caravaggio, the budding genius and tough-guy poseur, stared at a lot was himself. When, in 1645, an inventory was made of his few possessions it included, along with sundry weapons and a guitar, '*un specchio grande*' – a large mirror. Now studying yourself in a mirror was in fact a requirement of any artist wanting to master the *affetti*, the passions, to rehearse expressions that could then be used in history paintings. And since at the turn of the 17th century there had been a new emphasis – in music and poetry, as well as in visual art – on extreme feeling, such as horror, pity, adoration, shock, fear and sorrow, painters who wanted to experiment with an art of high emotion would do best to rehearse the attitudes and body language on themselves. That was one reason Caravaggio had done his lizard-bite.

It may be that mirrors helped Caravaggio focus his images, but it's also apparent that they helped him focus his mind. For they appear – along with self-images – over and over again in his work, functioning sometimes as an emblematic shorthand for the power of art itself, sometimes as the instrument of self-knowledge. That's why the most famous, desirable and dangerous prostitute in Rome, Fillide Melandroni, appears beside an image-less convex mirror as Mary Magdalene, the fallen woman on the point of conversion. She sees through this glass darkly to her salvation. But if art's for redemption, it's also for vanity. That's why Caravaggio poses the self-infatuated Narcissus gazing adoringly at his own face reflected in the stream. The compulsion to create a mirror image, to duplicate life, is at the root of art, but the tragically cautionary story tells of the worm of self-admiration gnawing at that root.

So it's not surprising that, in 1597, Caravaggio turned a commission from del Monte for a gift to his old patron, Duke Ferdinando de' Medici, into a literally stunning manifesto on the power of the image. The decapitated, snaky-coiffed head of the female monster, the Gorgon Medusa, whose gaze turned men to stone, was a standard motif in European courts. Everyone knew the myth of the hero Perseus, protected and equipped by the goddess Athena with a mirrored shield that, when held up to Medusa, froze the monster in her own horrified gaze long enough for him to slice off her head. No self-respecting princely warrior could be without his own shield or helmet or breastplate engraved with the head of Medusa, the sign that he too would stun his enemies into submission. But the story had a sequel that had been taken as the founding myth of the arts, since Pegasus, the flying steed of Perseus, had dipped his hoofs in the blood of the Gorgon and struck them into the ground of Mount Helicon, from which the fountain of the Muses then sprang. The wellspring of art was the blood of the monster.

When you put all that learning together with the fact that the most famous illusionistic shield-painting of Medusa's head had been done by Leonardo da Vinci and had, until lost some time in the late 1580s, been owned by the Medici, it's obvious that del Monte himself assigned Caravaggio the job of making a replacement gift for the Duke. The chance of competing with, and even perhaps outdoing, Leonardo was, of course, irresistible to Caravaggio, all of twenty-six, and he rose spectacularly to the challenge. His *Head of Medusa* was not just another virtuoso display of illusionism. It became a complicated, brilliant statement on the force of images.

Looks can kill, the painting says to us. This one certainly did. The stagey genius of Caravaggio, the peerless virtuoso of shock-horror, makes sure *we* feel the lethal surprise, for when we look at the painting we are seeing exactly what Medusa saw: self-image as death warrant. The first shudder happens. We get to survive, though, to admire the optical trickery of the artist. For although Caravaggio is actually painting on a bulging, convex, circular poplar-wood shield, he's used deep shadow to make it appear the opposite: a scooped concave bowl from which the ghastly head of Medusa more violently protrudes. The face swells almost to the point of explosion, with brows knitted in disbelief; eyes popping from their sockets (as ours feel they are doing when we look at it); cheeks distended; and the razor-toothed orifice (the predictable site of male nightmares) gaping open, tongue lolling against the shiny teeth, mouth forever frozen in its silent scream.

The thing, the picture, is repellently both dead and alive. Since the painting captures Medusa at exactly the moment of death, her skin is still rosy with life. And although she is self-petrified, the serpentine perm from hell continues to coil, seething with defiant reptilian vitality even as the head on which the vipers sit perishes. Caravaggio is having a really good time doing this. The glistening, segmented bodies and scaly skin of the snakes are highlighted, the better to convey the endless writhing – heads turning this way and that, forked tongues flickering in and out of the light.

Then there is the oddly stalactitic spray of blood depending like a collar from beneath the neatly sliced neck. For a painter so peerlessly adept at rendering the precise properties of every substance, liquid as well as solid, the detail seems at first sight oddly unreal, or else perversely stylised. Given his tastes and his way of life, it's a safe bet that Caravaggio would have been present at some of the gory public executions that took place in Rome; probably at the most famous of them all, the decapitation of the Cenci women for having planned the murder of Beatrice Cenci's incestuous father (while her brother had his flesh torn from him). So the artist knew what bloodshed looked like. But the coagulated collar of spikes had a point. Del Monte the amateur alchemist and nonpareil know-all would have known the tradition dear to physicians by which the blood of the Gorgons was also said to have been the origin of coral, used as a potent curative medicine and as a talisman or amulet worn round the neck to protect the wearer from evil and harm. It's a perfect theme for Caravaggio: life brought from death.

The theatre of cruelty was everywhere in Rome: not just decapitations, but public burnings of heretics, such as Giordano Bruno, and the grim weekly display of felons hanging from gibbets. Caravaggio was close to this violence. Now he was officially part of the Cardinal's household he could carry a sword, or rather have a boy servant carry it for him. This didn't prevent the police from trying to arrest him for wearing a weapon without a licence, provoking from Caravaggio a rather grand statement of his rights as a member of del Monte's retinue.

He was leading two lives, and they were not always kept strictly apart. On the one hand he was the privileged, famously gifted painter of the Cardinal, doing ceiling paintings for his suburban villa and much sought after by other Roman grandees. But he was also the unpredictable, sword-carrying, dagger-wielding eccentric with the hair-trigger temper. When his brother Giovanni Battista came to the Palazzo Madama to seek him out (hoping, the innocent, to encourage him to marry and have children), the painter flatly denied having a brother at all! Bewildered and, presumably, hurt by this repudiation, Giovanni Battista left without ever setting eyes on him. Then there was the company he kept: whores and courtesans such as Fillide Melandroni and her Sienese friend Anna Bianchini, both often cited by the law for violent assaults. Despite the fact that there had been specific Church bans on the painting of women of ill repute, especially in sacred history paintings, Caravaggio repeatedly and lovingly used them as models. The whole power of his art, after all, turned on his utter determination to give physical presence to what had previously been wan stereotypes. So while shocked critics complained that a Magdalene was nothing more than a working girl drying her long hair, for Caravaggio that was precisely the point – especially since the learned would have remembered that, in her reborn life, Mary Magdalene had used her hair to dry the feet of the exhausted Christ in the house of the Pharisee. To have Fillide, the most scandalous teenage courtesan in the city, pose for a painting of Mary Magdalene, the orange blossom of her conversion held against her provocatively low and sumptuous décolletage, would not have been just an act of defiant nose-thumbing at the scruples of the Church. Caravaggio was using the palpable presence of the worldly woman to make the force of her conversion even more dramatic. A make-up pot and comb lie discarded on the table, and the convex mirror remains dark, save for a square patch of brilliant reflective light – the light that makes Caravaggio's art possible and gives hope of a redeemed life to the sinner.

Caravaggio might have won an argument with the frowning fathers about posing a courtesan as the Magdalene, but it was even more outrageous to use Fillide as the sainted *Catherine of Alexandria* beside the spiked wheel of her martyrdom, her index finger toying with the edge of what must have been Caravaggio's own duelling rapier. It was the complete opposite of the customary image of the saint as pallid, angelic virgin. She exudes power, even danger. This Catherine's eyes glitter as sharply as the weapon. But, if pressed, Caravaggio could turn any suspicion of indecency back on the obtuseness of the questioners. Why were the saint's throat and neck so conspicuously bare? To remind worshippers of her beheading, naturally! Why was she clad in the sumptuous velvet and embroidered damask that seemed more likely to be the kind of dress in which Fillide received her high-born Florentine lover and protector, Giulio Strozzi? Remember that Catherine was a princess, the picture of resolute calm, not of eye-rolling terror – someone, in other words, to reckon with!

Whatever mutterings there may have been about the liberties that Caravaggio took, del Monte at any rate ignored them, knowing that his star painter was in the process of creating an entirely new kind of Christian art: more palpably dramatic and emotionally direct than anything that had been produced since Michelangelo. So when it became urgent to find an artist to paint the two side walls of the Contarelli Chapel in the church of San Luigi dei Francesi, just over the road from the Palazzo Madama, del Monte, who had the job virtually in his gift, knew exactly where to turn.

## VI

IT WAS CARAVAGGIO'S moment and Rome's, the two of them fitting like a hand in a glove. Pope

Clement VIII's Holy Year of 1600 was fast approaching: a year of fervour, pilgrimage and grace, when absolution would be extended, indulgently, to sinners who normally would have been denied salvation – sinners like Caravaggio. But the Holy City itself needed respite. Caravaggio was a palazzo boarder, but he knew, every day and in every pore of his skin, the other Rome, the city of a hundred thousand dirt-poor, ravaged by plague, burdened by taxes to pay for the Pope's sorry little wars, bellies never full, watching the harvest and praying for a good one to make bread and pasta affordable. When the Tiber flooded in 1598, smashing the Ponte Santa Maria, later nicknamed the Ponte Rotto (Broken Bridge), it seemed as though Rome was in need of wonders.

And it was about to get them. The chapel whose walls had been assigned to Caravaggio was in the French church of San Luigi. The history to be painted was that of St Matthew because a French cardinal, Mathieu Cointrel, had made a bequest for his saintly namesake to be venerated, and had left elaborate, detailed instructions on how the scenes – of martyrdom and the calling of the tax collector by Jesus – should be handled: how many figures, the setting, and so on. The ceiling vault had been done in 1593 by Giulio Cesari, now known grandly as the Cavaliere d'Arpino, quite possibly with the young Caravaggio's help. But as Rome's favourite history painter, d'Arpino had been in constant demand and had failed to finish the rest of the chapel. The Superintendence of St Peter's had taken over responsibility for its completion and had handed the task to del Monte, who had nodded in Caravaggio's direction.

The opportunity must have been both exhilarating and terrifying. The *Matthews* would be by far the biggest paintings he had ever done, both in physical size and in public visibility. Everything he had painted up till now had been under his control, even when, like the *Medusa*, it had been for a special commission. Those works had been easel paintings, done directly from nature in his studio under strong light; pictures for which he determined the number of figures and their disposition within the space. Now, though, he had to conform to Cointrel's specifications and even perhaps to d'Arpino's precedent on the ceiling: a crowd of figures, saintly radiance, grandiose architecture, deep space. And he also knew that he might have done genre scenes and still-lifes and tarts dressed as saints to perfection, but this job would be the making or breaking of him.

So Caravaggio set to work on *The Martyrdom of St Matthew* slaughtered beside his altar on the instructions of the Ethiopian king. He tried to fulfil the requirements of the deep architectural space of the church in which the murder had been committed: the massed extras, the translation of the martyr at the moment of death – and, perhaps for the first time in his life, he seized up. The instructions felt like chains. Caravaggio didn't do deep space, and he certainly didn't do a big cast of characters. The entire force of his dramatisation depended on proximity, not distance; on compression, not expansive grandeur. It was all about direct, personal identification. How could the beholder identify with a crowd?

The more he tried, the tighter those confining specifications gripped, weighed him down. So, for the moment, Caravaggio gave up on the martyrdom and broke free to work on the left-hand facing wall where he had greater conceptual liberty to paint *The Calling of St Matthew* not least because the lines in the Gospel referring to this life-changing moment were so terse: 'And as Jesus passed from thence, he saw a man, named Matthew, sitting at the seat of custom: and he saith unto him, "Follow me". And he arose, and followed him.' The idea made sense to Caravaggio, who for his own reasons specialised in the possibility of redemption coming to the most unlikely and hardened sinner. Inspiration came as easily and as quickly to him as it had proved unattainable for the martyrdom: here he could paint what he knew; paint from nature; paint a scene from the actual life of Rome, the life he lived and that all those who saw the painting could immediately recognise.

So he took the table and one of the boys from *The*

*Card Sharps* and set them down in a low dive with a high ceiling, filthy walls and an oil-paper window with one of the panes torn – the damage, of course, exquisitely rendered. The scene would have been instantly familiar to anyone coming into the chapel: the flash dressers; the table; the chink of coin being counted; receipts being checked; hard men and soft boys. They knew those low-end places. Caravaggio's genius for counter-intuitive vision was roaring along on all cylinders. And then, having broken one rule – the noble setting – why not break the biggest one of all? Instead of a composition where everything turns around the conversionary encounter between Christ and the tax collector, he made the episode seem, at first sight, almost incidental. We aren't presented with the group transfixed by the moment – some of the figures don't even see Jesus and St Peter coming through the doorway. One of them is slumped over the table and the money; his elderly neighbour, the spectacles an emblem of his moral as well as visual shortsightedness, doesn't bother to look up. Two customers with beards coming through the room? What do they want? Someone deal with them – tell them thanks, but we're busy.

Then Caravaggio takes this tease of understatement just about as far as it can go. Rather than making Christ the centre of the painting, he obscures him, the better for the beholder to seek him out.

Theologically, the move is perfect – especially for a Holy Year in Rome – because St Peter comes visually between us and Christ, just as he did institutionally through the papacy. But the move works psychologically as well, since the partial view of Christ's body concentrates attention on the one unmissable feature: the extended right arm with its pointing finger. It's the perfect union of the sacred and the profane – which is, after all, the heart of the story. The gesture is borrowed from the most famous passage of painting in Rome, a moment of sacred inception: God the Father's fingertip touch to Adam on Michelangelo's Sistine ceiling. From the pointing hand – rather than from the dirty window – comes a bolt of light, the light of the Gospel, flooding the face of the cherubic page-boy who ought not to be down here mixing with this scum anyway, and who seems ever so slightly to flinch from the light, his arm resting on Matthew's shoulder, instinctively and endearingly self-protective. The shaft of light travels on to the disconcerted features of Matthew himself, his cheeks suddenly flushed at being found out, and who answers the holy summons with a move that every Roman, every pilgrim would have recognised: 'What? *Me?*' It's possible, as some scholars have argued, to read the direction of the gesture as 'Don't you mean *him?*' – the slumped figure to his right. But to me there's no doubt that it's the bearded man who's about to become Matthew the apostle, for the richness of his dress, Caravaggio's own favoured black velvet, makes the conversion to humility all the more telling.

Something else has happened. For once Caravaggio isn't interested in direct eye contact between his characters and us: the gesture would be too cheaply ingratiating. What we do is come upon the scene as hidden witnesses, privileged eavesdroppers out there in the darkness of the chapel. And the fact that the figures are close to life-size makes the illusion of just happening on that very moment all the more heart-stopping.

Riding his confidence, knowing *The Calling* had worked, Caravaggio went back to *The Martyrdom*, feeling less shackled by Cointrel's list of specifications. He didn't ignore them entirely, however: the canvas is, by his standards, crowded, but instead of shrinking his characters within a deeply recessed and grandiose architectural setting, he brings the action almost unbearably close to our faces. Instead of some lofty church, there are a few stone steps to suggest an altar, along with a fleeing choirboy. And Caravaggio has thought hard about the way in which the two great paintings on facing walls emotionally rebound on each other. After the uncanny silence and stillness falling over *The Calling*, *The Martyrdom* is a pinwheel of chaos, the figures flying out centrifugally from the one adamantly fixed figure of the nude assassin. It was typical of Caravaggio to make the only still figure, the muscled nude at the fulcrum of all this gesticulation, the embodiment of evil. His outstretched arm gripping Matthew's wrist so that he can strike again (a rivulet of blood, this time painted realistically, is already spurting through the martyr's white robe) is the satanic pair to the extended arm of Christ on the opposite wall. In another stroke of theatrical genius, a moral tug of war is going on. Matthew's expiring body is sinking into what seems to be a black baptismal pool, his left arm and hand foreshortened as if gesturing in our direction for help. But down swoops the angel towards him, bearing the martyr's palm in the hand that will also carry him to his heavenly reward.

Which leaves us mortals somewhere in the middle, floundering, shrieking (for this is as noisy a painting as *The Calling* is quiet), the strobe lighting flickering from body to body and face to face to maximise the panic. But at the back of the crowd (the same notional distance behind the action that we are in front of it) someone pauses in flight. Sweaty, dishevelled, hair matted, brows knitted, Caravaggio casts himself as the cowardly sinner, knowing that he should, for the sake of his own skin, get away from the scene of the crime, and fast too – but at the same time he can't not look. His only saving grace is that he holds a lantern. He is, after all, and against his nature, the bringer of light.

## VII

THE CONTARELLI CHAPEL *Matthews* of 1601 made Caravaggio. Even foreign artists and writers, such as the Dutchman Karel van Mander, knew about his achievement. But they also knew about his equally famous shortcomings:

*There is a certain Michelangelo da Caravaggio who is doing extraordinary things in Rome . . . this Michelangelo has already overcome adversity to earn reputation, a good name and honour with his works . . . But one must take the chaff with the grain; thus he does not study his art constantly . . . [but] after two weeks of work he will sally forth for two months with his rapier at his side and his servant boy after him, going from one tennis court to the next, always ready to argue or fight, so he is impossible to get along with . . . This is totally alien to art.*

Not, however, to Caravaggio's kind of art: contact painting, the kind that burst right through the canvas, obliterating the protective threshold of distance and depth in order to come and get us. It's an art in which all the niceties of decorum were contemptuously ignored and aesthetic slumming was unceremoniously kicked out of the door. The ruffian poor, to whom all those Fathers of the Church paid lip service, were now actually featured at the centre of the action instead of being relegated to socially entertaining bit parts – to the role of the token destitute on whom redeeming miracles were graciously performed. Although it would have been (and still is) more convenient for the dignity of art to imagine the delinquent Caravaggio – wounded in fights, sometimes giving as good as he got, and keeping deplorable company – as an entirely different person from the maker of stupendous sacred paintings, the truth was that the latter could not have existed without the former. The genius was the thug.

But he was *such* an unmistakable genius that the rich and the mighty lined up to protect him from the consequences of his misdeeds. As they saw his star rise, so they began to pay him more and to compete for his services. Paradoxically, it was precisely Caravaggio's use of live models from the streets – the habit that made him notorious to the academicians of San Luca and elicited denunciations for leading impressionable young painters astray – that helped make the grandest churchmen feel they were somehow bringing into being an art of renewed Christian humility. Caravaggio's all-too-evident familiarity with the world of the poor was a particular virtue in Holy Year, when Church leaders, in imitation of Christ, were supposed to be washing feet, embracing misfortune and anointing sores. Cardinals on the whole didn't go in for much sore-anointing. Now Caravaggio could do it for them – he could be their virtual slummer for Christ.

The idea must have especially appealed to Tiberio Cerasi who, as Treasurer-General to Pope Clement, was immensely wealthy and wanted a funeral chapel (he died while it was being decorated) in the church of Santa Maria del Popolo. At the edge of the Piazza del Popolo, the church was the first that pilgrims entering Rome from the north would have visited, so Cerasi would have known that his chapel would be seen by the multitudes. He was determined, then, to hire only the very best; and to show that in this context he could unite opposing factions he assigned the altarpiece to Annibale Carracci, the favourite of the pro-Spanish Farnese family, and the walls to Caravaggio, attached to the pro-French del Monte.

Caravaggio signed the contract even before he had finished *The Martyrdom of St Matthew*. This gave him a mere eight months to do another major piece of public work, something that would prove the Contarelli paintings weren't just a flash in the pan. But the fact that the only painter he considered a serious rival – Annibale Carracci – was also involved in the project must have been a spur. So many of his strongest paintings had been kick-started by the works of artists whose company he aspired to be in: the lost

Leonardo Medusa; d'Arpino's vault paintings for the Contarelli Chapel; and now he was to share the stage with not just the greatest member of the Bolognese Carracci dynasty, but the one most praised for his naturalism. Ironically, though, at this time Annibale had never been less earthy. His edge was softening, his colours brightening; his lode-star was evidently now Raphael's classicism. So his *Assumption of the Virgin*, c. 1590, was all winsome and wholesome: a golden-haired Madonna borne aloft by the power of pure cheerfulness, peekaboo seraphs peeping from her skirts, apostles acclaiming the show with grandiose gestures. Caravaggio's paintings on the other hand – another martyrdom (*Peter*) and another conversion (*Paul*) – offered bituminous darkness lit by lightning-strength glare. If the *Assumption* was effortless uplift, these were earth-rooted, tensed with pain and labour, weight and work, grunting and groaning. As if he needed to, Caravaggio rubbed home the difference by echoing the outstretched arms of Annibale's *Virgin* in the out-flung arms of Paul as he receives the light of faith. But he is flat on his back, his eyeballs burnt by the epiphany.

Yet there had been another false start. Initially, daunted (as with *The Martyrdom of St Matthew*) by what he'd taken on, Caravaggio produced a strangely overburdened and wooden *Conversion of St Paul* which the Fathers responsible for the Cerasi Chapel rejected. And, as with the Contarelli Chapel, a setback had the effect of concentrating Caravaggio's creative intelligence. The rethink must have begun with the space itself, much narrower and more confining than the Contarelli Chapel. All the instincts of post-Renaissance art were to respond to spatial confinement by using perspective to open up the space. With the theme of Mary's ascent to heaven, Annibale had naturally followed this precept, so his painting was full of bright light. But Caravaggio's best moments were often counter-intuitive. Instead of trying to defeat the cramped room optically with smaller figures and illusions of deep space he did exactly the opposite, bringing his massive figures of men and beasts right to the very picture edge so that, immense and lumbering, they seem, alarmingly, about to fall into our personal space. A shoed hoof, a meaty derrière, the sharp edge of a shovel and a chapped elbow are pushed right in our face. Instead of relief and depth, we get holy claustrophobia.

How it works! Witness was never closer, the distance between observer and event never more successfully annihilated. We are positioned right beneath the inexorable, grinding, wheel-like machine of men hoisting Peter, who considered himself unworthy to be martyred in the same position as Christ, to his upside-down crucifixion. The genius of the thing is that it's not a done deed, but a permanently relentless *doing*: a heaving and lifting, yanking and cranking that seems to go on and on for ever, which is of course how the Church wished believers to experience it, especially in St Peter's own city. It also wanted ordinary people to feel implicated in the sin at the same time as feeling assured of salvation if only they remained obedient to St Peter's successors. So Caravaggio gives us the people of Rome as they had never been seen before in sacred art (the Carracci certainly had never dared put them there): bulky bodies, filthy calloused soles, faces in darkness (they have not yet seen the light), to divert our attention to the straining force of muscle, tendon and knotty veins. However, the effect of imagining the crucifixion as, first and foremost, manual labour, emphasised by the glint at the edge of the shovel, is not to damn the labourers but to have us identify physically with them. And to identify too with their victim, the apostle whose head is one of the greatest of Caravaggio's achievements: mouth opened in a moan to register the pain of his pierced hands, eyes expressing acceptance and – the most stunning detail of all – wisps and strands of fine hair flying away from the side of his head as he is hoisted to his consummation.

If the Peter of the Piazza del Popolo is – aptly enough – all about the people, the Paul is all about power. Both pictures are deceits for Christ: the ancestor of the rich and grandiose popes represented at the moment of his greatest humility; and the unswerving embodiment of the faith militant represented at the moment of prostrate impotence, thrown from the saddle of his worldly power to persecute. With the latter, Caravaggio has a moment of blinding insight of his own, parting with centuries of Pauline iconography, including his own earlier version of the saint, as the usual bearded elder. Caravaggio thinks instead of the local cops: young, brutal, stubble-chinned, strapping swaggerers like the *bravi* he fell foul of all too often. Taking years off Paul, of course, only makes the stunning force of the light that had thrown him all the more potent. It's a *literally* dazzling conceit.

Once again, Caravaggio isn't separating his own life from his art, but rather bringing his gift for raw-boned heft to his one-man revolution in sacred painting. He uses the narrow space and our viewing angle to force us *down*, as if he were pushing us bodily to the ground (he had lots of practice) so that we find ourselves beneath the piebald's raised hoof. Instead of the routine angels that crowded his first effort, there are just three characters: horse, groom and floored apostle. But as with *The Calling of St Matthew*, the shock of the painting is in the light that floods over the horse's body and bounces back from Paul's torso and face so that its strength reflects in the heavily veined leg and creased forehead of the gentle groom, enfolding him too in its saving illumination. The attributes of Paul's worldly power are broken: plumed helmet thrown off, armour straps unfastened, and the eyes that had sought out Christians to harass are now an extraordinary yellow, as if the cornea had first been scorched by the light, then covered, as the Gospel says, with a filmy cataract. Blinded, he will in three days be rewarded with the first true sight of his life.

## VIII

FOR A FINE, SUNLIT moment, around 1601, Caravaggio must have felt invincible. Cardinals were fighting for his services. Some time that year he agreed to work for another wealthy cleric with a worldly eye, Ciriaco Mattei, and may have moved into his palazzo, although he is still said to have been with del Monte in October. It wasn't beyond Caravaggio, revelling in the competition, to swap studios just when the mood took him. The more outrageous he became, the better his patrons seemed to like it. For Marchese Vincenzo Giustiniani he did the kind of full frontal Cupid no one had ever seen before – not on canvas, at any rate. He's supposed to come from the world of the gods, but was an Eros ever so here-and-now? He's a full-frontal pubescent street kid, with tousled hair, juicy lips and a wicked grin, as though he knew that the divine attributes – those clip-on eagle's wings and the prop arrows – had been rented (like him?) for the day. So it takes an act of absurdly willed primness to insist that this *Amor Vincit Omnia (Love Conquers All)* must nonetheless be a high-tone allegory, celebrating the patron's cultural virtuosity: the musical instruments and score; the architect's T-square and compass; the hero's armour. Yes, the score and the T-square display a 'V' for Vincenzo (and virtuoso), but that's also the letter formed by the boy's spread thighs on their rumpled sheet, with the hairless little spigot-willy plumb in the centre. No wonder the picture was kept behind a green silk curtain, although whether Giustiniani did so for prudence or for the mischief of a staged revelation to chosen guests we'll never know.

What's on display is Caravaggio's way with surrogate touch. The tip of Cupid's own wing brushing the outside of a creamy thigh is an invitation to experience secondhand the delicate caress. But at the same time that he could do these visual soft porn teases, Caravaggio could make the physical exploration of touch the expression of impeccable theology. Was not the heart of the Christian mystery, after all, the incarnation of the son of God, his presence made manifest in flesh? To truly believe, then, meant to press that flesh.

So for the touchy-feely Vincenzo Giustiniani Caravaggio also painted the most shocking *Doubting St Thomas* ever made in Christian art. All decorous euphemisms are abandoned. The proof being in the probing, Christ's hand with the stigmata on its back steers the horny finger of Thomas deep into the lipped, almond-shaped wound in his own body, burying it up to the joint. The filthy nails and rough skin of the apostle make this penetration both invasively shocking and sacrificially tender: almost, one is tempted to say, akin to the equally probing intimacy of the sexual act. Revelation and belief are written in the arched eyebrows and creases of Thomas's brow, and in the clinical intensity of the stooped apostles' transfixed gaze, as if they are observing a medical procedure. To make true believers, Caravaggio's picture says, it's not enough to direct the eyes; you must also register the spectacle viscerally, on your flesh. Hairs should stand up on the neck; goose-bumps rise on the skin.

It's not that Caravaggio is a wilful demystifier, rather that his mysteries and miracles happen in the here and now; and in the presence of ordinary people seen close up and unbeautified, their clothes worn and torn, their hands and feet grimy, their mouths agape, their brawny limbs flung about. It was one thing for the priesthood to utter pieties about the renewal of Christian simplicity, of washing, in imitation of the Saviour, the unwashed; it was quite another for a painter to rub their noses in the unsavoury reality of the street poor. But then Caravaggio was truly unique in being the only painter in Rome whose life actually bridged the world of the cardinals' palaces and the great churches and that of the gambling dens, whorehouses and wine shops of the *popoli*. To be able to bring the one world to the other was his great gift to the Church, but it came with risks.

Sometimes they paid off. The church of Sant' Agostino, for instance, commissioned Caravaggio to paint a *Madonna of Loreto* celebrating the village to which the Virgin's house (complete with Madonna and Child) had been miraculously airlifted. Loreto had long since become a place of mass pilgrimage for the humble and credulous, and images of the Virgin usually featured her seated on the roof of the airborne house. Caravaggio is in no mind to break the spell; rather, by bringing it so firmly down to earth – to the doorway of a Roman street, in fact – he wants to maximise its closeness to the lives of the pilgrims. So the Madonna hasn't just landed in the Roman countryside; she's picked up the genes. She has the voluptuous form, thick black hair, olive skin, heavy eyelids and Roman nose of a local beauty – in fact Caravaggio's local beauty, his model and mistress Lena Antognetti. Her Jesus is to scale: a sweetly pot-bellied *bambino* of the kind that Roman mothers still worship, though less sacramentally.

The conversion of the Madonna from ethereal to earthy, however, is the least of the painting's original qualities. Always thinking about the bond with the viewer, Caravaggio had yet another of his outrageous insights. Instead of *assuming* beggar-pilgrims kneeling at the feet of the Virgin, why not actually feature them doing so, thus once again stripping away the threshold between our world before the image and the world within it? Pilgrims can be imagined coming to this painting, looking at it from below (for that's the way Caravaggio has angled the viewpoint) and seeing before them their painted brother and sister mendicants, complete with the rough, torn feet of the wayside. The Virgin's own balletically turned white foot balancing on its heel only serves to emphasise the grimy ones of her devotees, all corns and calluses. Presented to us so graphically that we can practically smell them, those feet are the kind of detail meant to be edited out of art, especially art dedicated to the higher devotion. But for Caravaggio there can be no higher devotion than the reverence of the footsore.

Those feet passed muster. Two other pairs did not. The first of these, huge and burly, were even more aggressively confrontational than those of the pilgrims of Loreto, and they were intended for one of the most dignified commissions that had come

Caravaggio's way: the altarpiece that would complete the ensemble of *Matthew* paintings in the Contarelli Chapel. Caravaggio had been asked to replace an unsatisfactory sculpture by another hand of St Matthew being inspired by an angel to write his Gospel. This third painting would, in effect, make the Contarelli Chapel his own, eclipsing his old master d'Arpino whose ceiling vault would vanish into insignificance. But, perversely (since the saint was hardly depicted that way in *The Calling of St Matthew*), Caravaggio made him into a clod whose doltishly bewildered expression and ungainly tramp's feet thrust out aggressively into the beholder's space. Aghast at the affront, the St Peter's office responsible for completing the chapel rejected the painting. This was the second time (after the *St Peter* in the Cerasi Chapel) that this had happened to the man who had become a *pittore celebre*, an acknowledged 'famous painter', but he took the blow on the chin and painted the tamer alternative still to be seen in the Contarelli Chapel.

For the first time, too, the word 'indecent' was uttered in connection with the 'maestro'. In August 1603 Cardinal Ottavio Paravicino described his paintings as somewhere (dangerously) 'between sacred and profane'. But if Caravaggio overheard these murmured reservations, it hardly slowed him down in his headlong determination to humanise the Gospel. Given that the church of Santa Maria della Scala in Trastevere was located in one of the poorest quarters of Rome, where the clergy were famous for pastoral care among the working people, Caravaggio might have thought that his unvarnished approach to *The Death of the Virgin* would be sympathetically received. His conception of the piece was shockingly simple. Traditionally, the period following the Virgin's death had always been thought of as a mere sleep or 'dormition' prior to her ascent to paradise. As such, Mary was preserved from the corruption of mere humanity. Just as her conception of the Saviour had been immaculate, so her departure from the world was similarly fleshless. The trouble was, Caravaggio didn't really do fleshlessness; he did flesh; and in this case, unambiguously dead flesh – the body, it was said, of a drowned prostitute (*meretrizia*) from the brothel quarter of the Ortaccio, fished out of the Tiber. So beneath its red dress Mary's body is crudely bloated; her skin is greenish, and yet another pair of feet have been left offensively bare and, of course, none too clean.

The painter was out to provoke not shock, but rather pathos and grief. This unequivocally dead Mary allowed him to render the expressions of the apostles – miraculously gathered round her bier after their dispersion – and the lamentation of Mary Magdalene as authentically tragic. If the Virgin were merely suspended in a sacred snooze pending her translation to heaven, the grief might seem disproportionate. Yet faced with a true death, a definitive exit from the world, the crushing sense of loss becomes credibly overwhelming. But the Fathers of Santa Maria in Trastevere, horrified by the indecencies, didn't see it that way. The painting came down, to be bought for the Duke of Mantua five years later by Peter Paul Rubens, who was so spellbound by its emotional intensity and so apparently bent on vindicating Caravaggio that he exhibited it for a week before having it sent to Mantua.

## IX

It was Caravaggio's third rejection. Not so long ago it had been he who was turning jobs down. Now he could ill afford to lose them. But as the pace of new commissions slowed, the tempo of his assaults and imprisonments in the Tor di Nona speeded up. When not in jail he was living in shabby rooms in the Campo Marzio, with just a few sticks of furniture, his swords and daggers, guitar and fiddle, and a dog he called 'Crow', whom he taught to do a party piece, walking on its hind legs. In his fancy, but torn and filthy, black velvet Caravaggio cut a figure of elegant menace, stalking the mean streets around the Piazza Navona with tough-guy mates, such as Onorio

Longhi. The *sbirri*, the papal police, knew him only too well for his short fuse and his relish in brandishing his blades and screaming insults at passers-by, especially if they happened to be painters whom Caravaggio had written off as pathetic mediocrities and parasites – which is to say pretty much everyone except himself, his pals and the select few, such as Annibale Carracci, whom he truly respected. 'We'll fry the balls of scum like you' was one of the choice items of verbal abuse sent the way of one of his victims, who probably got the feeling, as he looked and fled, that the *cervello straniere* – the crazy-brain – just might do that!

How could the *pittore celebre* behave so outlandishly? How could he not? Caravaggio was all of a piece. The animal aggression; the in-your-face invasion of body space; the revelling in outrage, sexual and social; the embrace of the socially unwholesome; the shameless self-dramatisation that made him come at you out of the blackness, in a bolt of violent light; the cocksure sense of invulnerability that somehow also went along with compulsive self-implication – all this was what made him, at the same time, the most necessary, but also the most explosively uncontrollable, painter that Rome and the Church had ever taken on. It needed him for the same reasons that, in the end, disgraced and destroyed him.

And Caravaggio himself was incapable of riding

his fame to respectability and reliability. It wasn't enough that (even with the setbacks of the rejections) he had succeeded; he needed to take down the mediocre competition, especially if they had had the gall to land commissions from which he had been excluded. The worst, apparently, was Giovanni Baglione, who went around wearing a gold chain of honour and had been hired to paint a Resurrection for the Gesù, the new showplace church of the Jesuits. Although Baglione thought enough of Caravaggio to write a later biography that, given their relationship, is surprisingly even-handed, the esteem was definitely not mutual. Some time in the late summer of 1603 Baglione's follower Tommaso Salini, known to everyone as 'Mao', had been handed some verses about the two of them that, it was implied, were doing the rounds. They weren't exactly Great Poetry, but then they didn't need to be to get this kind of message across:

> *. . . Giovan Bagaglia, you're just a know-nothing*
> *Your pictures are just daubs*
> *I warrant you won't earn*
> *A brass farthing with them*
> *Not enough for cloth to make breeches*
> *So you'll have to go around*
> *With your arse in the air . . .*
> *Maybe you can wipe your arse with them*

*Or stuff them up Mao's wife's hole*
*So he can't screw her any more with his big mule's prick*
*Awfully sorry I can't join the chorus of praise*
*But you're quite unworthy of the chain you wear*
*And a disgrace to painting . . .*

And more in this vein. Mao showed them to Baglione, and in September 1603 Baglione sued the likely authors, Caravaggio and his friend and fellow artist Orazio Gentileschi, for libel. During the trial they were both locked up in the Tor di Nona, which would soon become home from home for Caravaggio. The evidence against him was circumstantial (no one had seen him actually write them or dictate them to the friends who probably did), but no one was fooled. His defence could best be described as enigmatically unrepentant. He claimed disingenuously never to have heard or seen any verses or prose, in Latin or Italian, that attacked Baglione, although evidently he made no secret of the fact that he rather approved of the views they expressed, saying that no one he knew rated Baglione at all. Asked whom he *did* rate, Caravaggio produced a list of those he considered 'skilled'. It included Annibale Carracci, d'Arpino and, rather surprisingly Federigo Zuccaro, the erstwhile dean of the Academy of San Luca and the epitome of empty refinement.

The trial rolled on inconclusively for months,

during which Caravaggio and Gentileschi remained first in jail and then under house arrest pending judgment. A great deal of evidence was presented about boys allegedly hired by Gentileschi and Caravaggio to distribute the verses, but nothing conclusive was decided.

In any event, this risk of a serious jail sentence (or, worse, time in the galleys) failed to cramp his style. The next eighteen months saw Caravaggio in and out of the Tor di Nona, his short temper getting him into trouble repeatedly. In April 1604 at the Moro tavern a waiter named Pietro da Fusaccia put a plate of eight artichokes, four cooked in butter, four in oil, in front of him. 'Which is which?' asked Caravaggio. 'No idea,' said Fusaccia. 'Why don't you smell them?' Perhaps it was the way he said it. 'Listen, *becco fottuto*, fucked-over cuckold, do you think you're talking to some *barone*, some bum?' Evidently it was a rhetorical question. Caravaggio threw the plate at the waiter's face and, so Fusaccia said, started to draw his sword. That weapon-happy impulse got him into further trouble with the *sbirri*, who twice stopped him. After he satisfied them that, as someone protected by the Cardinal, he was entitled to carry a weapon, the officer let him go, but he made the mistake of wishing Caravaggio a good night – to which the reply was, '*Ho in culo*' – up my arsehole. Off he went again to the Tor. In July 1605 he was arrested again for breaking into the house of two women, Laura and Isabella, and smashing its windows

Later that month, while standing in the Piazza Navona, a notary called Mariano Pasqualone was attacked from behind with what some said was a hatchet, others a sword. Although he lost a lot of blood, Pasqualone somehow survived. The assailant, dressed in a black cape, fled into the darkness. But no one was in much doubt about his identity. Pasqualone had made the mistake of worrying about the virtue of Caravaggio's model and girlfriend, Lena Antognetti, who was said to 'stand in the Piazza Navona' – which presumably meant that there wasn't in fact much virtue to worry about. But Pasqualone, smitten, went to her mother, explained about the long modelling sessions her daughter had with the notorious artist and promised to make an honest woman of her. The mother went to see Caravaggio. And Caravaggio went – we can safely surmise – berserk. Words were exchanged between the two men on the Corso, Caravaggio fuming that, since Pasqualone refused to wear a sword, he was unable to challenge him to a duel. So as an alternative he took direct action, in the Piazza Navona, and then fled all the way to Genoa where he was offered commissions to paint for aristocratic villas. No matter what Caravaggio did, no matter what appalling crimes he managed to commit, there would always be *someone* prepared to turn a blind eye if they could get their hands on one of his paintings. It was just as well. When he got back from Genoa he found that his landlady, Prudenzia Bruna, had locked him out and had his few belongings confiscated with a view to a sale that would cover his six months' arrears of rent. Caravaggio's reaction was to break her windows and to threaten to break her.

He was a homicide waiting to happen, and in May 1606 it did. Caravaggio and his crowd had had run-ins before with the Tomassoni brothers from Terni, sons of the captain of guard of the great papal-aristocratic clan of the Farnese. Gian Francesco Tomassoni was the *caporioni* (ward boss) of the area around the Campo Marzio, and his younger brother, Ranuccio, was a swaggerer with a crew of tarts, famously skilled with dagger and sword, and possessed of as much attitude as Caravaggio. Police reports, court statements and Caravaggio's early biographers disagree about the precise cause of the fatal quarrel: some say (since the violence took place near the tennis courts on the Via della Scrofa) that it was all about a game or a bet; others that this was just a convenient location to settle a row after Caravaggio took offence at something Ranuccio had said about his girl, probably Lena. At all events, the fight was a classic all-out Roman rumble between two small gangs: the Tomassonis against Caravaggio and a friend, Petronio Troppa, who was a Bolognese 'captain'. It ended when Ranuccio took a slashing wound, after which Caravaggio stuck him – depending on how we read the reports – in the belly or in the groin. Tommasoni was taken to his house near by, where he bled to death. Caravaggio was himself badly wounded but managed to escape, hiding out in the hills of the Roman countryside with benevolent and powerful protectors, probably the Colonna family, among whom were his old patrons the Marchese and Marchesa of Caravaggio. It was probably the Colonnas who smoothed his way in the autumn of 1606 to the Spanish territory of Naples. The papal authorities had proclaimed Caravaggio subject to a *pena capitale* – literally a price on his head – so it was urgent to get him beyond the reach of their police or any eager bounty hunters.

He stayed in Naples for nine months, turning out dark and stunning altarpieces, such as *The Flagellation of Christ* and *The Seven Works of Mercy*, 1606–7. The Neapolitan altarpieces are conspicuous for their compassion and tenderness, even – or especially – in *The Flagellation*, where our pity is touched through the enactment of unsparing, almost unhinged, cruelty. Caravaggio was already something of a name when he arrived in the city, and through this succession of powerful, sombre works became more so. In Naples there were generous patrons, a string of commissions and – *mirabile dictu* – no fights and no spells in prison. It seemed possible, for a while in late 1606 and early 1607, that he would stay, obliging the devout merchants, financiers and ennobled bureaucrats of the port city, steadying his talent and his temperament and making them work in tandem for the greater glory of God and himself.

But nothing was ever quite that simple for Caravaggio. The following year found him in Malta, the island fortress of the Holy Order of the Knights Hospitaller of St John. Through the Marchesa of Caravaggio, he secured an introduction to the Master of the Order, Alof de Wignacourt, who held out the possibility that on the island he might not merely have his crime overlooked but become a Knight himself. Caravaggio's social status as the son of a master builder and steward had always been ambiguous: neither evidently genteel, nor exactly bourgeois. Other Roman painters, such as d'Arpino, liked to flaunt their status as *cavalieri*. Now the fugitive murderer would be transformed into a Knight of St John and thus be made untouchable.

X

ON 14 JULY 1608 the black cape with the eight-pointed white star of the Order of St John was set over Caravaggio's shoulders and, being compared to the first painter of antiquity, Apelles of Cos, he was formally proclaimed a 'Knight of the Obedience'. Along with the honour came, thanks to the Grand Master, a gold collar and two slaves. Normally Caravaggio's crime – known to Wignacourt – would have been an insurmountable obstacle, but the Grand Master had the knighthood of talented non-nobles in his personal gift; he had applied to the Borghese Pope Paul V for an exemption in Caravaggio's case, and it had been duly granted. In the months between his arrival in October 1607 and his elevation Caravaggio had vindicated his reputation with portraits of Wignacourt and another Knight of the Order; a greenish snoring baby purporting to be a Sleeping Cupid (more clip-on wings); and an intensely moving *St Jerome*, his torso twisted in the act of writing, and a skull, a crucifix bearing the Saviour and a candlestick – one of Caravaggio's great still-life ensembles – lying on his plain wooden table.

But it was with *The Beheading of St John the Baptist* that Caravaggio effectively paid for his admission into the Order. At seventeen feet wide it was not just the biggest painting he would ever make, but incomparably the greatest – perhaps the most moving, profound and complex history painting of the 17th century. And the reason it was all those things was that Caravaggio had so personal a stake in its display of calculated murder, sacrifice and rebirth – so personal, in fact, that he signed his own name in its new form as Fr (*Frater*, that is Brother of the Order) Michelangelo. And he signed it in the gushing blood of the Baptist – thus transferring, with his brush, his own identity from murderer to martyr.

The oratory, whose eastern wall Caravaggio's painting almost fills with its over-life-size figures, was not just a place of ceremony and prayer. Beneath the floor were buried those who had died fighting the good fight against the Turks, who occupied virtually the entire eastern Mediterranean. So the oratory was, among other things, a mausoleum of chivalric martyrs, and the John (himself slaughtered at the whim of an oriental despot) that Caravaggio was painting for them would thus have specially sacred significance. But it was also, as Caravaggio would have known, the courthouse of the Order where delinquent Knights were tried and, if convicted, condemned. Behind the far wall would have been, at the time Caravaggio was working there, the cell in which the prisoners were held.

So even by Caravaggio's standards, an uncanny liquidation of the boundary between art and life was enacted in his painting. It wasn't just a matter, as in the Contarelli Chapel, of sustaining the illusion of a continuous space that the beholder could enter without the obstacle of a framing threshold to cross. The grimly empty prison yard where the scene of chilling horror is being enacted and across whose stones the martyr's blood is spilling is, as the art historian David Stone recognised from old prints, the same site used to hold and execute judgment on criminals. Push the logic further, though, and the Knights in whose name that justice was carried out would be in the position of Herod and Salome's slaughterers. So, notwithstanding Caravaggio's need to please his masters and brethren in the Order, a ribbon of ambiguity runs through this enormous painting, scheduled for completion by the Feast of the Decapitation of St John the Baptist on 29 August 1608.

And that ambiguity is, not least, about art itself. For, with the exception of the anguished old woman holding her hands over her head – or perhaps her ears to avoid hearing the order to saw through the Baptist's neck – the semicircle of figures represents a fiendish inversion of the traditional personifications represented in art. The heroic nude (like the very similar figure in *The Martyrdom of St Matthew*) is a ferocious butcher, gleaming blade behind his back; the figure of gravity and authority, the grizzled prison officer, is the implacable and impatient agency of decapitation; and the embodiment of beauty, her exquisiteness concentrated in the delicate flesh tones of her exposed arms, is the trophy-carrier of murder. And as with all his very greatest masterpieces – the Cerasi *Peter*, for example – Caravaggio has integrated into his conception the element of time: the figures constitute a chain of action that, since it is yet to be initiated, becomes completed in our own horrified imagination and so goes on and on in an unsparing *perpetuum mobile* of savagery. It's the extreme quietness with which this horrifying spectacle ineluctably proceeds that turns it into a true nightmare, a horror in which evil is permanently frame-frozen. There are no histrionics. The painting says bleakly: in places like this, this is just what happens. And we are, through the rolling centuries, meant to know what he means by places like this. The painting may have been made for the Knights of St John in the summer of 1608, but assuredly, to anyone who goes to see it in Valletta, it is not only for the anachronistic crusaders.

It was also made for the two prisoners corkscrewing their necks through the barred lunette window in the otherwise bare right side of the painting; which is to say for Caravaggio himself (whom I suspect may be loosely represented in one of their faces) and for us. For the notional distance behind the picture plane from where they are making their attempt to rubberneck the scene is pretty much the same as ours in front of it. What they represent is confinement and impotence. In fact, those keys hanging from the officer's belt, one of which I had held in my hand, are, as the classical tradition had it, the *claves interpretandi* – the keys of understanding. The power of this art is a confession of the limits of all art. A masterpiece painted at the very highest pitch of all Caravaggio's skills is nonetheless a confession of impotence before the beautified barbarism it pictures.

Except in one respect: that of the ultimate meaning of the martyrdom itself, a foreshadowing of the redemptive sacrifice of Christ, and thus the means, through the shedding of blood, to rebirth. Who would better understand the urgency of that expiatory sacrifice than a convicted murderer who had himself been given the precious chance – through this very painting – of exactly such an opportunity of another life? The blood sprays, as it had done with the *Medusa*, and from it comes the same kind of coralline coagulation that turns an act of evil into one of healing. The source of art, as with Medusa, becomes the source of life. No wonder, then, that as it flows over the ground, it forms itself into Caravaggio's *new* name, the name of his redemption: 'Fr Michelangelo'.

Which should be the end of the story, should it not? But of course it can't be. Caravaggio, who had just painted one of the most sublime outcries against cold power, was unable to arrest his own hot temper, and barely four months after being admitted to the Order got involved in an altercation with a fellow Knight. Imprisoned in solitary confinement, he managed (suspiciously) to climb out of his twelve-foot-deep dungeon with the help of a rope, and then to find a boat conveniently waiting to take him due north to Sicily, his next place of refuge. Had he been captured and sent for trial, he would then, as a delinquent Knight, have been incarcerated in the very cell that he had painted in *The Beheading*! On 1 December 1608 the Knights gathered in the oratory to hear that, although he had been summoned four times, Caravaggio had failed to appear before their tribunal. He was therefore 'expelled and thrust forth like a rotten limb'. Above the Grand Master as he pronounced the sentence would have been the greatest thing Caravaggio had ever done. It was no mitigation.

## XI

HE WAS IN sicily for a year. An old friend from the rat pack days in Rome, Mario Minniti, who'd posed with fruit and lute for Caravaggio, was now the Great Painter in Syracuse and would have helped with both commissions and hospitality. But Minniti couldn't have done much to give Caravaggio what he needed more than anything else: peace, pardon, rehabilitation. If his reputation followed him on the run, and gave him work, so did his offences – and they gave him no respite. His jumpiness shows in the big Sicilian altarpieces, done at Syracuse and Messina to which he moved. Lately art historical revisionists, over-eager to correct anything that smells of romantic melodrama, have tried to make the case that Caravaggio's Sicilian works aren't a descent from the inspirational summit of the Malta *Beheading* or the Roman paintings of his glory years, but are just different: darker, quieter, if anything more soberly touching. It's not an entirely perverse over-correction. In *The Burial of St Lucy*, 1608, *The Adoration of the Shepherds*, 1608–9, and *The Raising of Lazarus*, 1609, there are passages of profoundly moving, chastened simplicity. But while it's possible to read the sketchier, brushier technique that Caravaggio has adopted for these paintings as evidence of a deliberately simplified manner, that judgment too is the result of romantic projection. It's just as likely that some of these rougher works are simply unfinished; Caravaggio may well have been hurrying to complete them because, with increasing desperation, he needed to. Aside from their almost monochrome wan-ness, what they almost all have in common, big as they are, is a sense of the action being re-enclosed inside a frame: hushed and impenetrable, sealed off behind the picture plane from the devotee. This was a new way of painting for Caravaggio all right. But it was not a better way.

The fact of the matter was that in Sicily he was jumpy and unsettled, and with good reason. The list of those with scores to settle had grown. Whatever it was that he had done in Malta, whomever he had offended (if not the whole Order), he had just added formidable enemies to his pursuers. His only chance for salvation lay with the possibility of pardon back in Rome. That was where he wanted to be and where his art was meant to hang. And somehow he heard that, such was the faith in his making of marvels, there were indeed well-placed eminences working on just such a pardon: Cardinal Francesco Gonzaga and, still more decisively, Cardinal Scipione Borghese, the art-loving nephew of Pope Paul V.

So in October 1609 Caravaggio sailed north again in the direction of that hope, returning for prudence's sake to Spanish Naples. The fact that his old patron-ess, the Colonna Marchesa of Caravaggio, the woman who had first introduced him to the art world of Rome, was also then in Naples, at her villa in Chiaia, could hardly have been a coincidence. The Marchesa was a link with Rome, perhaps a bridge to his longed-for pardon. His earliest benefactress would be his latest, perhaps last, chance as the brilliant arc of his career descended now into the glittering bay.

Which may be why his guard was down as he was leaving the Osteria Cerriglio on 24 October. For at that moment he was jumped by unknown assailants, his face mutilated and his body so badly beaten that he was left for dead. News of his supposed death was sent to friends and patrons, who must have been shocked but not surprised. Who, then, would want

Caravaggio dead? More to the point, who did *not* want Caravaggio dead? First there were the artists in Rome whom he'd abused verbally and physically; then Mariano Pasqualone, the notary whom he'd done his best to kill in the Piazza Navona; the powerful and well-connected Tomassoni family who had lost a son and brother to his sword; and more recently the injured party in the Maltese affray who, through the artist's escape, had been denied redress and judgment?

But there were also people who wanted him alive, and working for the Church and for themselves. So the paintings that Caravaggio did as he was convalescing amidst the jasmine and lemon trees of Chiaia (although the attack had been so violent that his face and body never seem to have really recovered) were in some sense his vindication, a demonstration that, though he'd been inches from death, he could still turn on the old magic. The brushy gentleness of the Sicilian altarpieces was banished again. Instead there was a return to his sharpest, most brilliantly dramatic manner, yet this time without even a hint of flash. These paintings, some of them done for the men who would get him his pardon – especially Scipione Borghese – were images of redemptive suffering and, yet again, decapitation, as if he couldn't get the image of his own *pena capitale*, his capital sentence, out of his mind. There was an excruciating martyrdom of St Andrew, face agonised; and another head of St John the Baptist, this time on a platter, with a conspicuously ungleeful Salome pensive rather than jubilant at her dubious trophy. It was as if Caravaggio wanted to give the victors pause. For the shepherd boy hero in his *David with the Head of Goliath,* is likewise wistful, the most conflict-ridden David ever to be imagined in either marble or paint.

This went against the grain. But then Caravaggio's whole career, his whole life, had gone against the grain. He had been a brute, but one capable of devout sublimity. The worst things he had done, the blood he had spilt, defied belief, but the best things he had done on canvas had always been designed to summon it. So now, on the edge, as he must have hoped, of a resurrection from the bloody mess at the Osteria Cerriglio, he turned everything upside-down yet again in a bid for understanding – not just from the cardinals and the Pope, but from us, and perhaps from himself.

In the work of other hands – not least the other Michelangelo – David had embodied the union of godly virtue and heroic strength, the qualities the Florentines liked to imagine they saw in themselves and their city when they passed the great statue on the Piazza della Signoria. And since in Christian tradition David was the ultimate progenitor of Christ, his depiction was also associated with the triumph of good over evil, of saving grace over satanic transgression. To see David, pure, heroic and divine, was to see what Christian art was *for*: beauty as the agency of salvation. So even if Michelangelo did not inscribe his own features on his statue, everything about his vocation, its God-touched genius, was invested in the perfection of the form. Others were more literal. In a painting that has not survived, Giorgione is known to have represented himself as David: Big George, the conqueror of pagan sin.

Now that would hardly be credible in Caravaggio's case, would it? And yet the exercise in role reversal is more complicated than it first seems. For could it be that, as others have argued, *David with the Head of Goliath* is in fact a double self-portrait? His youthful upper body washed with light, David is the blessed Caravaggio that *was*, the Caravaggio of his prodigious beginnings, the maker of Christian beauty (the slingshot of his conquest has been assimilated into the loose shirt tied about his waist, a piece of white fabric as exquisitely tactile as anything the painter had ever rendered). But that same light flows downwards on to the face of the ogre, the Caravaggio that *is*, the bisexual goat, the murderer, the immense encyclopedia of wickedness.

One of Caravaggio's earliest biographers wrote that the model for David was in fact his 'Caravaggino' – the 'little Caravaggio who lay with him', and in some literal sense this might be right; but of course it in no way precludes the deeper possibility of his being the painter's wishfully thought alter ego. They are bonded, the beauty and the beast, not least by the raking light that holds them both as tightly as David grasps Goliath's head. Instead of presenting the stark opposition between heroic victory and vanquished evil, they seem united by tragic self-knowledge. In fact, the distribution of virtues and vices in a painting that reaches to everything that counts most – sex, death and redemption – is surprisingly even. David's sword, as every commentator has noticed, points – indeed touches – his own groin (the place where Caravaggio finished off Ranuccio Tomassoni), while the shirt end hanging below his waist forms itself into an unsubtle phallic length. While the young David had been the personification of godly courage, notoriously the old King David was a lecher and a judicial murderer who sent to his death the inconvenient husband of the Bathsheba whom he coveted and took to his bed.

Nothing is as simple as it seems. There are no pure heroes, no irredeemable villains. For despite the unappetising drool, the bared teeth, the sallow skin and the hooded eyelids, what is so striking about Caravaggio's self-portrait is that – unlike himself as the decapitated Medusa – what he sees in the mirror, for the last time, is in fact not a monster but a man; evidently a man capable of monstrous things, but a man for all that. Even the entry wound – which, had Caravaggio wanted to make gory, we can be sure he would, is oddly abbreviated into the frown of a man who, at the moment of his death, is struggling to comprehend something significant. The Caravaggio-Medusa had been a testimony to the lethal art of reflection, but on her face is written the horror of denial. Goliath likewise seems to have been taken by reflection at the instant of extinction, yet somehow the knowledge survives the killing; for the head held by David is still disturbingly alive, the mouth open in a terminal bellow.

Once again – as with the spurting blood of Medusa and the blood of John as he lies on his fleece – the pumping spray from Goliath's severed neck is the substance of translation from evil to atonement; from unpardonable to pardoned sin; the baptismal medium of rebirth.

## XII

But to be shriven, absolved, reborn, Caravaggio first had to get to his pardon – to Rome. On 10 July 1610, encouraged by news of the progress of his cause, he boarded a felucca sailing north from Naples.

Then followed the famous denouement, so terrible that, were this not the life and death of Caravaggio, it would be unbelievable. The ship put in at the small port of Palo, just west of Rome, where the local commandant had either not heard of Caravaggio's impending pardon or mistook him for someone else. He was thrown in jail yet again, only securing his freedom by paying whatever money he could lay his hands on. By the time he was free the felucca had sailed north again, taking with it the parcel of paintings intended for the cardinals and patrons, especially Scipione Borghese. One of his biographers claims that he actually saw the ship sailing away, carrying his painted vindications with it. Desperate to retrieve his work, Caravaggio then attempted to follow the course of the felucca further north, away from Rome and up the Tuscany coast to the Spanish garrison town of Port' Ercole on the peninsula of Monte Argentario. Just how he got there is unknown. It was too far to walk, a horse would have cost him money he didn't have, and a donkey would have been far too slow. Besides, he was feverishly sick. Burning from the illness, he collapsed on the beach near Port' Ercole and was taken to the local hospital run by monks, where, as his biographer writes, 'without the aid of God or man he died as miserably as he lived'.

Some time later, Scipione Borghese would have uncrated the fine parcel of paintings that Caravaggio had made in Naples. Among them would have been *David with the Head of Goliath*. Now the Cardinal would have been quite used to Davids, and even more used to severed heads, which were a speciality of the day. But he would never have seen a head quite like this: a self-portrait of the painter, set in utter darkness, flooded only with the light of tragic self-knowledge. Some time, a long time before, Scipione must have been accustomed to hearing confessions. Now he was seeing one – one that implored absolution.

The *pena capitale* placed on Caravaggio four years earlier had promised a reward for anyone turning in the fugitive murderer's head. Now Caravaggio was, in the guise of Goliath, turning himself in. 'Guilty as charged', the head seems to say. 'Can I have my reward, my pardon, my rebirth now?'

'*Mi dispiace*,' I like to imagine the sympathetic Cardinal saying. 'Sorry; tremendously sorry, but you're too late.'

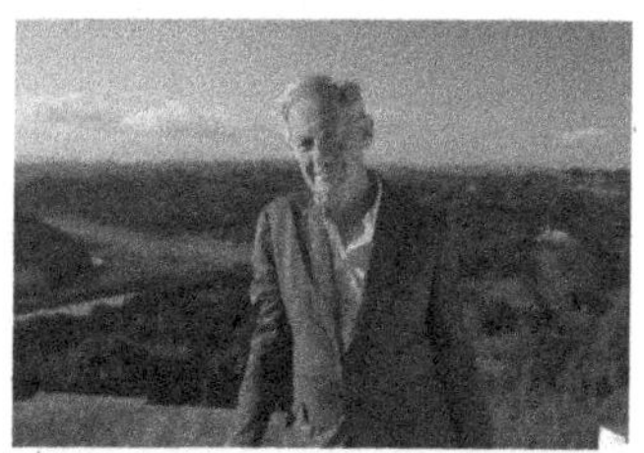

Simon Schama is University Professor of Art History and History at Columbia University. His award-winning books, translated into fifteen languages, include *Citizens, Landscape and Memory, Rembrandt's Eyes, A History of Britain, The Power of Art, Rough Crossings, The American Future, The Face of Britain, Wordy* and *The Story of the Jews: Finding the Words (1000 BCE – 1492)*.

His art columns for the *New Yorker* won the National Magazine Award for criticism and his journalism has appeared regularly in the *Guardian* and the *Financial Times* where he is Contributing Editor. He has written and presented more than fifty films for the BBC on subjects as diverse as Tolstoy, American politics, and *The Story of the Jews* and is co-presenter of the landmark series on the history of world art, *Civilisations*.

RECOMMENDED BOOKS BY SIMON SCHAMA

*Scribble, Scribble, Scribble: Writing on Ice Cream, Obama, Churchill and My Mother*
*The American Future: A History*
*Belonging: The Story of the Jews Volume II, 1492–1900*

# THE POWER OF ART

In *The Power of Art*, Simon Schama closes in on intense make-or-break turning points in the lives of eight great artists who, under extreme stress, created something unprecedented, altering the course of art for ever.

The embattled heroes – Caravaggio, Bernini, Rembrandt, David, Turner, van Gogh, Picasso and Rothko – faced crisis with steadfast defiance. The masterpieces they created challenged convention, shattered complacency, shifted awareness and changed the way we look at the world. With powerfully vivid story-telling, Schama explores the dynamic personalities of the artists and the spirit of the times they lived through, and traces the extraordinary evolution of eight world-class works of art.

‘Packed with noisy enthusiasm, punchy arguments and verbal agility’ *Independent*

# THE STORY OF THE JEWS: FINDING THE WORDS (1000 BCE – 1492)

It is a story like no other: an epic of endurance against destruction, of creativity in oppression, joy amidst grief, the affirmation of life against the steepest of odds.

The great story unfolded in these pages is not – as often imagined – of a culture apart, but of a Jewish world immersed in and imprinted by the peoples among whom they have dwelled, from the Egyptians to the Greeks, from the Arabs to the Christians.

Which makes the story of the Jews everyone's story, too.

'Inspiring . . . Schama tells it with panache, weaving facts and anecdotes into a vivid history' *Observer*

'Unforgettable . . . a delicious cacophony of conversations and clamorous arguments echoing across history' *Daily Telegraph*

## VINTAGE MINIS

The Vintage Minis bring you the world's greatest writers on the experiences that make us human. These stylish, entertaining little books explore the whole spectrum of life – from birth to death, and everything in between. Which means there's something here for everyone, whatever your story.

|  |  |
|---|---|
| *Desire* | Haruki Murakami |
| *Love* | Jeanette Winterson |
| *Marriage* | Jane Austen |
| *Babies* | Anne Enright |
| *Language* | Xiaolu Guo |
| *Motherhood* | Helen Simpson |
| *Fatherhood* | Karl Ove Knausgaard |
| *Family* | Mark Haddon |
| *Summer* | Laurie Lee |
| *Jealousy* | Marcel Proust |
| *Sisters* | Louisa May Alcott |
| *Home* | Salman Rushdie |
| *Race* | Toni Morrison |
| *Liberty* | Virginia Woolf |
| *Swimming* | Roger Deakin |
| *Friendship* | Rose Tremain |
| *Work* | Joseph Heller |
| *Money* | Yuval Noah Harari |
| *Austerity* | Yanis Varoufakis |
| *Injustice* | Richard Wright |
| *War* | Sebastian Faulks |

<table>
<tr><td align="right">Depression</td><td>William Styron</td></tr>
<tr><td align="right">Therapy</td><td>Stephen Grosz</td></tr>
<tr><td align="right">Drinking</td><td>John Cheever</td></tr>
<tr><td align="right">Recovery</td><td>Helen Macdonald</td></tr>
<tr><td align="right">Eating</td><td>Nigella Lawson</td></tr>
<tr><td align="right">Rave</td><td>Irvine Welsh</td></tr>
<tr><td align="right">Psychedelics</td><td>Aldous Huxley</td></tr>
<tr><td align="right">Art</td><td>Simon Schama</td></tr>
<tr><td align="right">Calm</td><td>Tim Parks</td></tr>
<tr><td align="right">Dreams</td><td>Sigmund Freud</td></tr>
<tr><td align="right">Ghosts</td><td>M.R. James</td></tr>
<tr><td align="right">Religion</td><td>Karen Armstrong</td></tr>
<tr><td align="right">Science</td><td>Ian McEwan</td></tr>
<tr><td align="right">Freedom</td><td>Margaret Atwood</td></tr>
<tr><td align="right">Death</td><td>Julian Barnes</td></tr>
</table>

vintageminis.co.uk